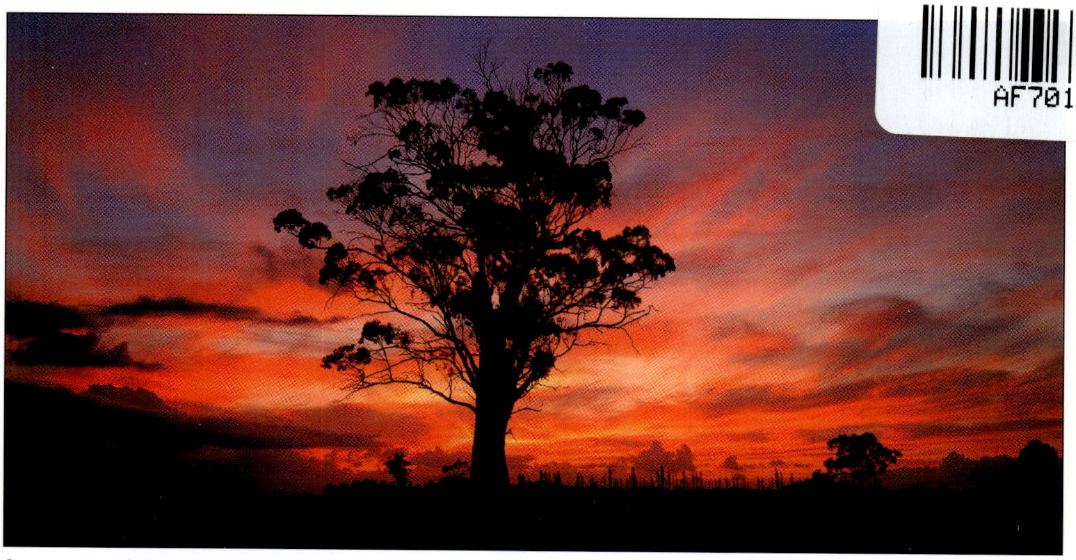

Sunset over farmland near Hagley.

On this island, you'll discover the creative spirit of artists and craftspeople inspired by clear southern light, by warm and mellow timbers, by the astonishing variety and beauty of the landscapes.

From city markets to fertile farmlands, from remote ocean coastlines to rugged highland peaks, from yesterday to today, Dennis Harding's photography captures the true spirit of this unique island.

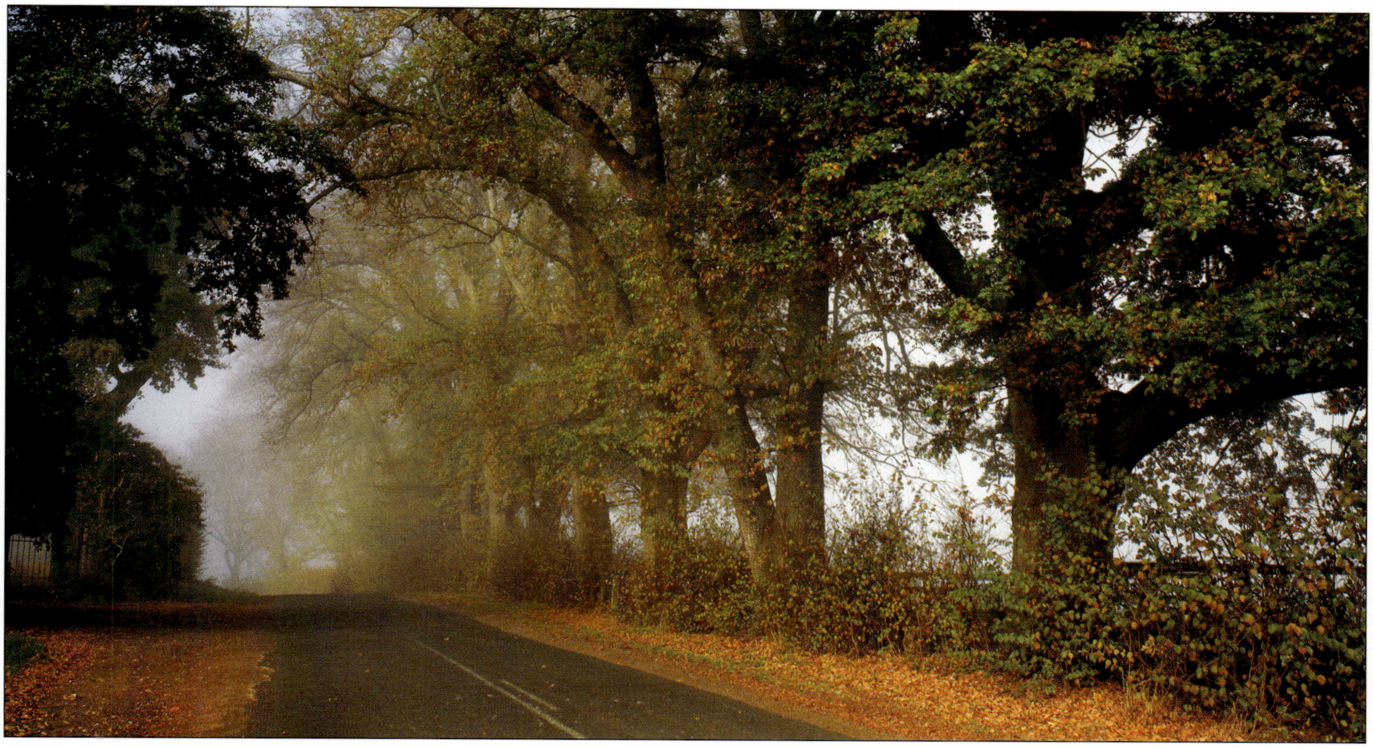

Autumn colours along Pateena Road.

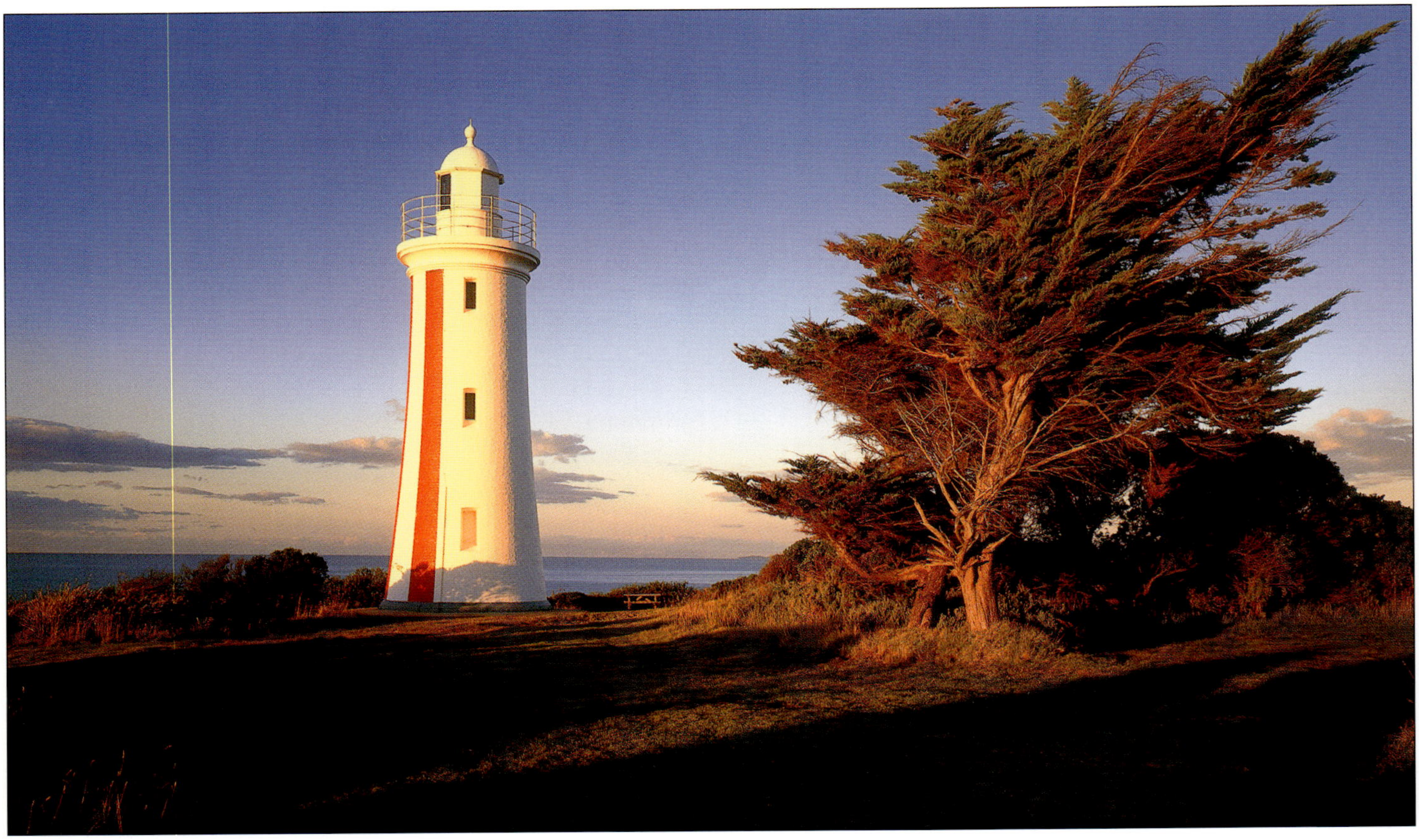

Sunset on Mersey Bluff Lighthouse, Devonport.

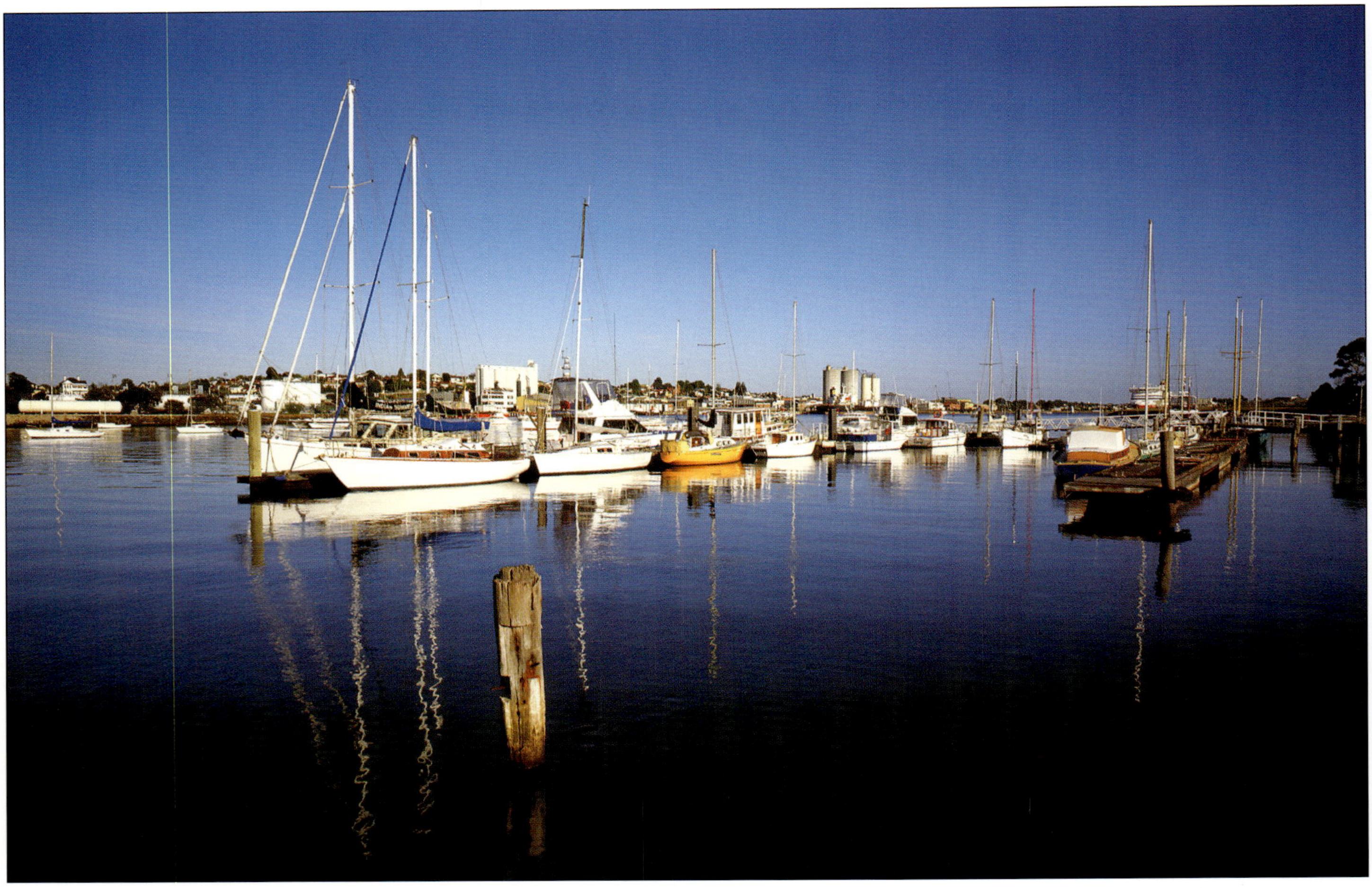

The Mersey River, Devonport.

The North

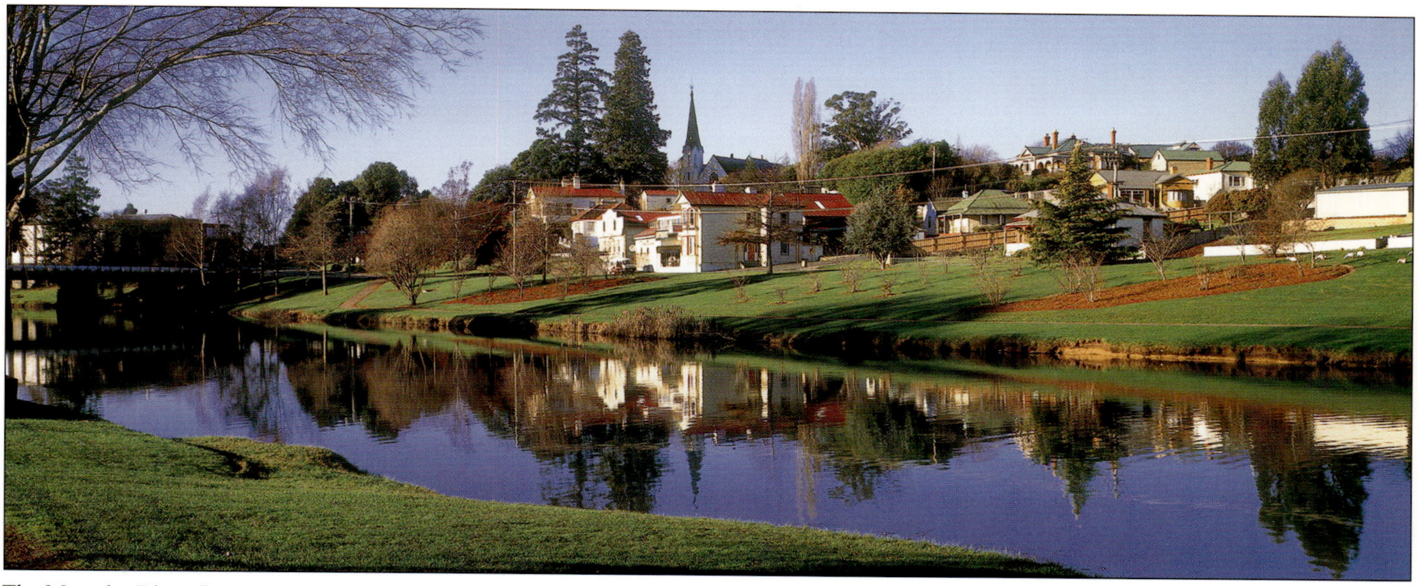

The Meander River flows though the picturesque town of Deloraine.

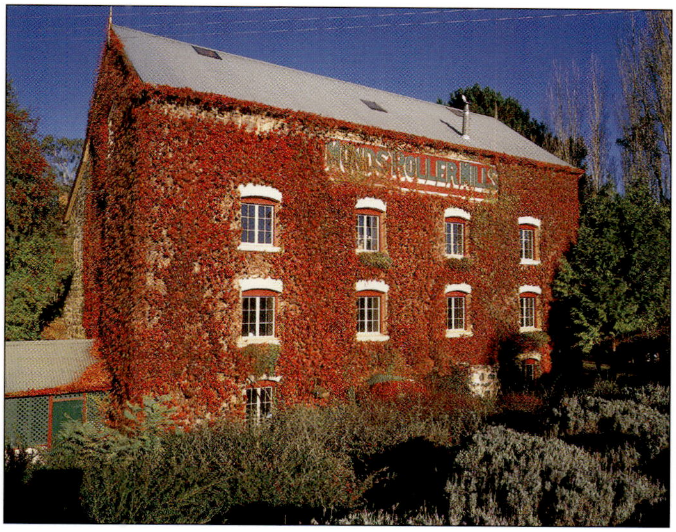

The Mill, Carrick.

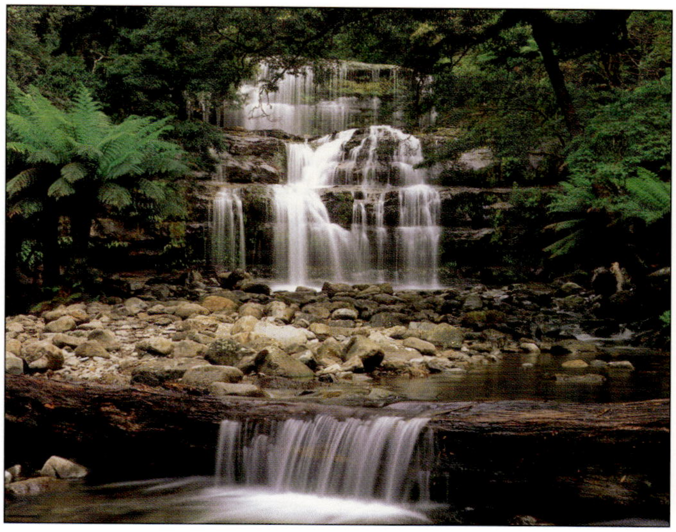

Liffey Falls.

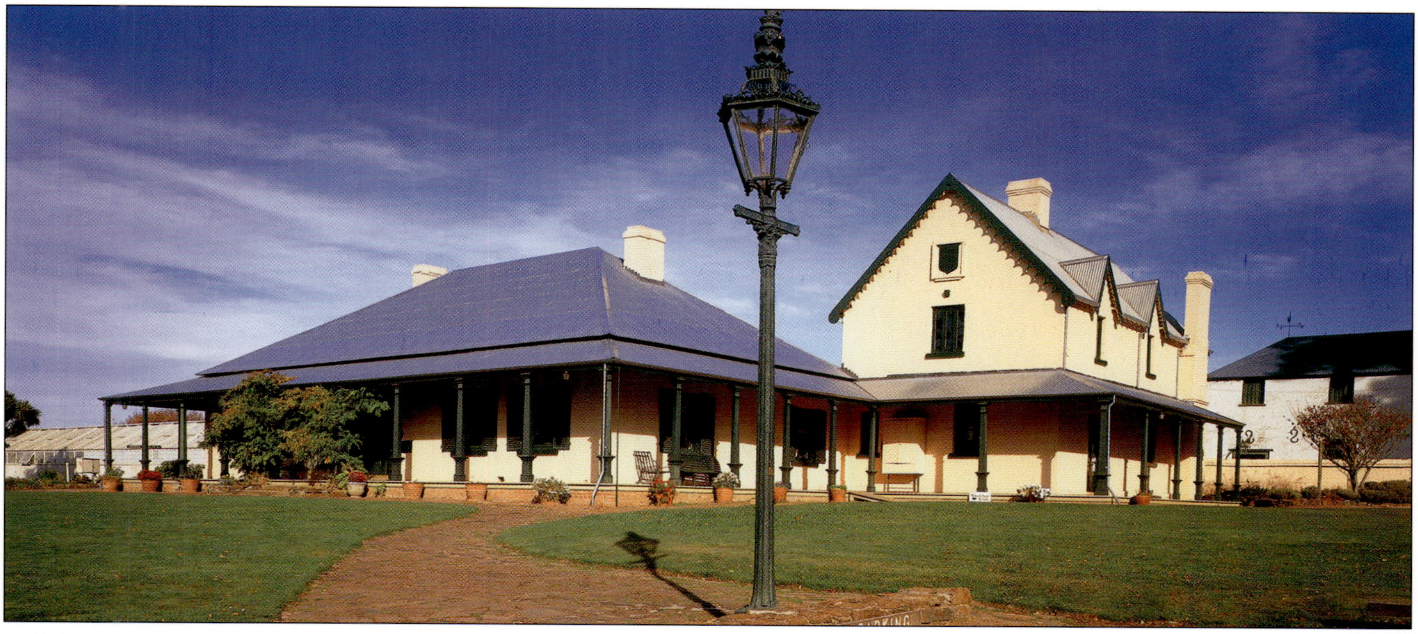

Built by Thomas Reibey in 1819, Entally House contains a rare collection of antiques.

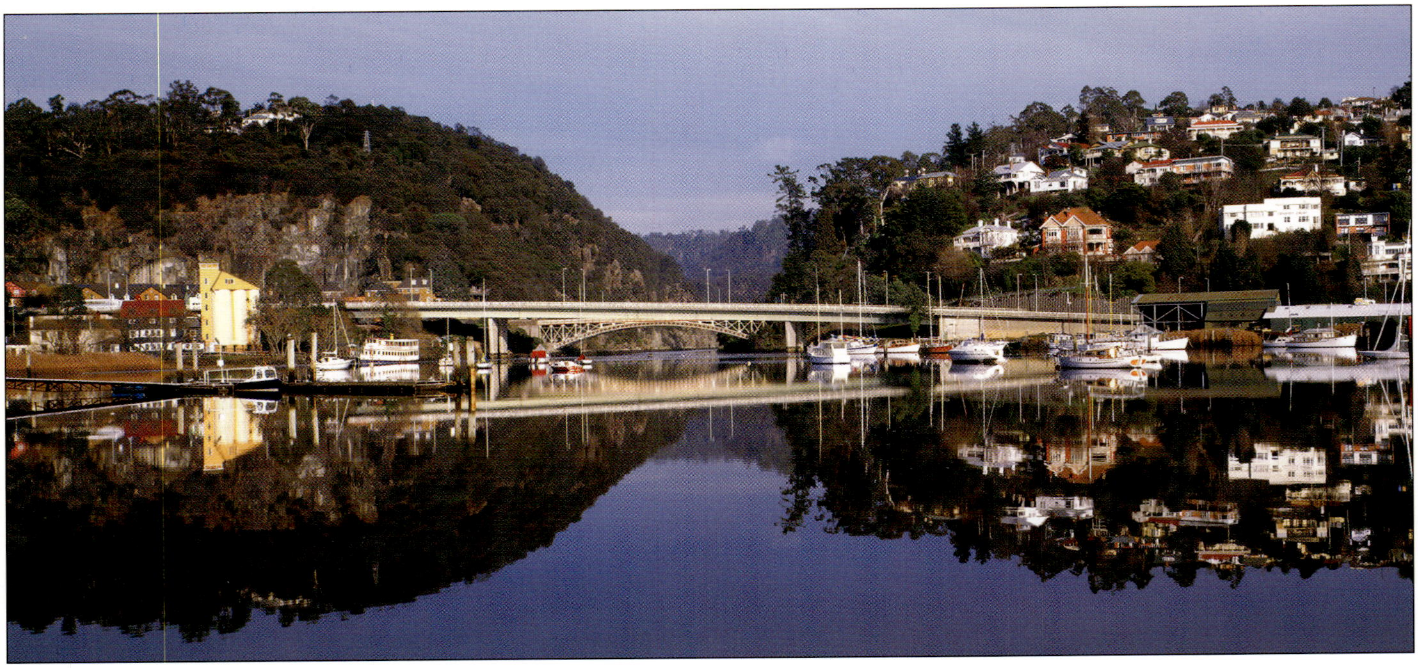

Picturesque reflections in the Tamar River, Launceston.

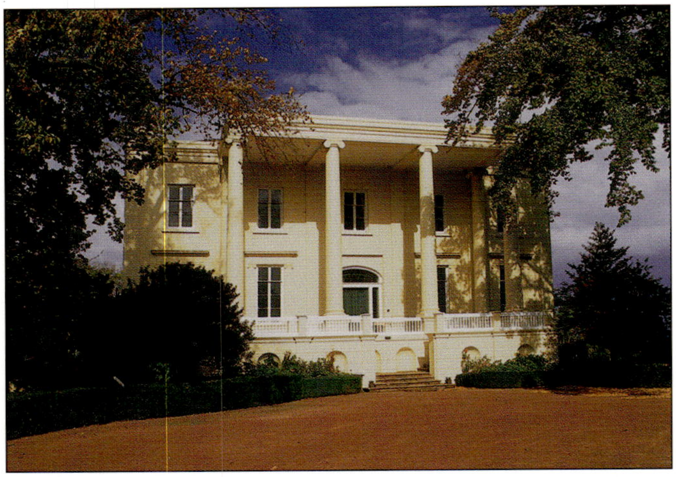

Clarendon Homestead (1838), at Nile near Evandale.

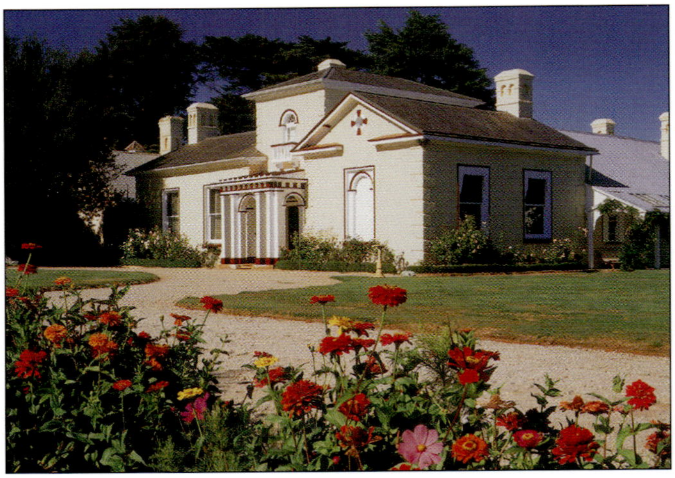

Woolmers Estate, a time capsule of Australian colonial history.

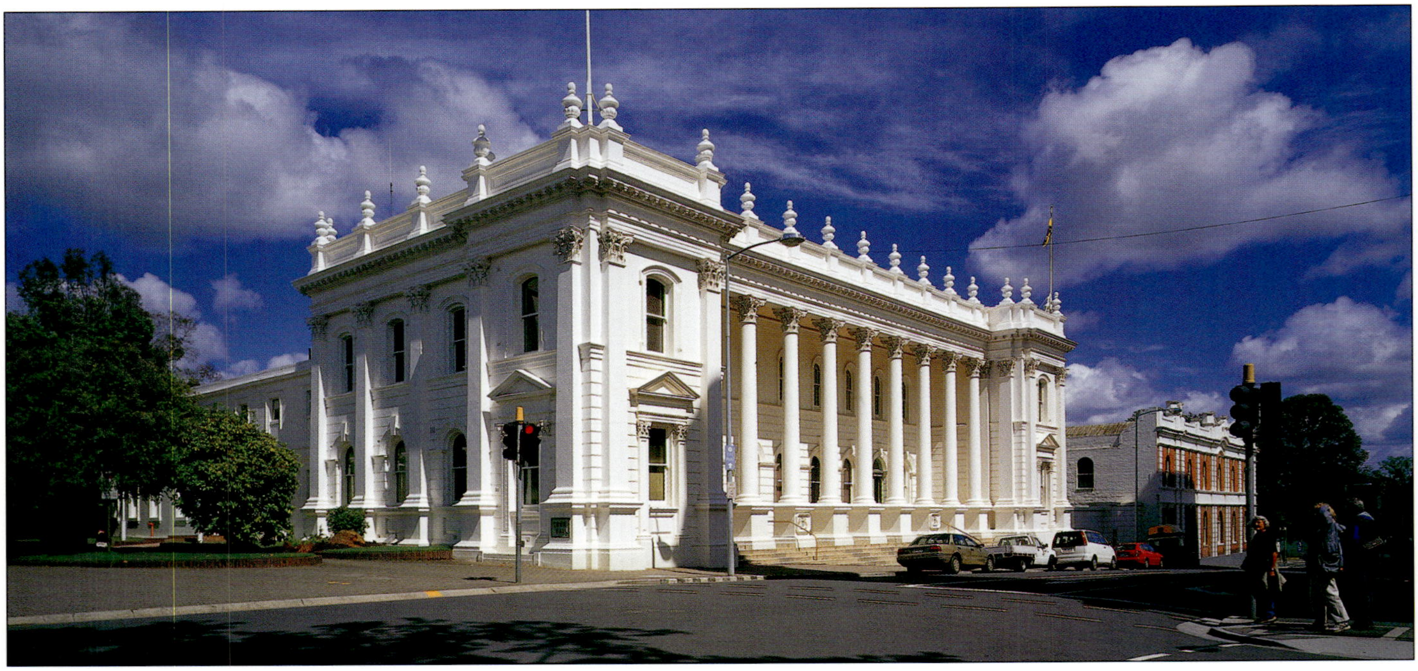

Launceston Town Hall, (1864).

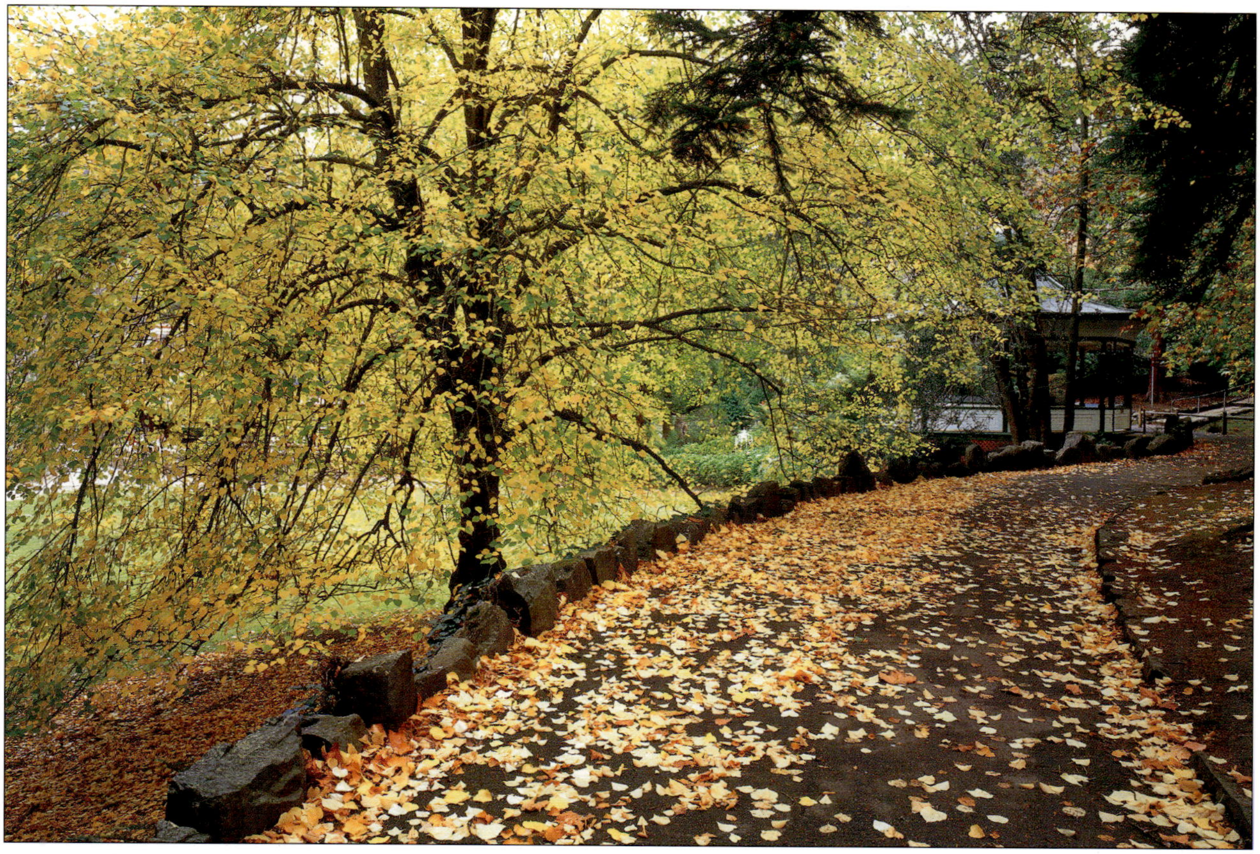

Autumn colour, Cataract Gorge Reserve, Launceston.

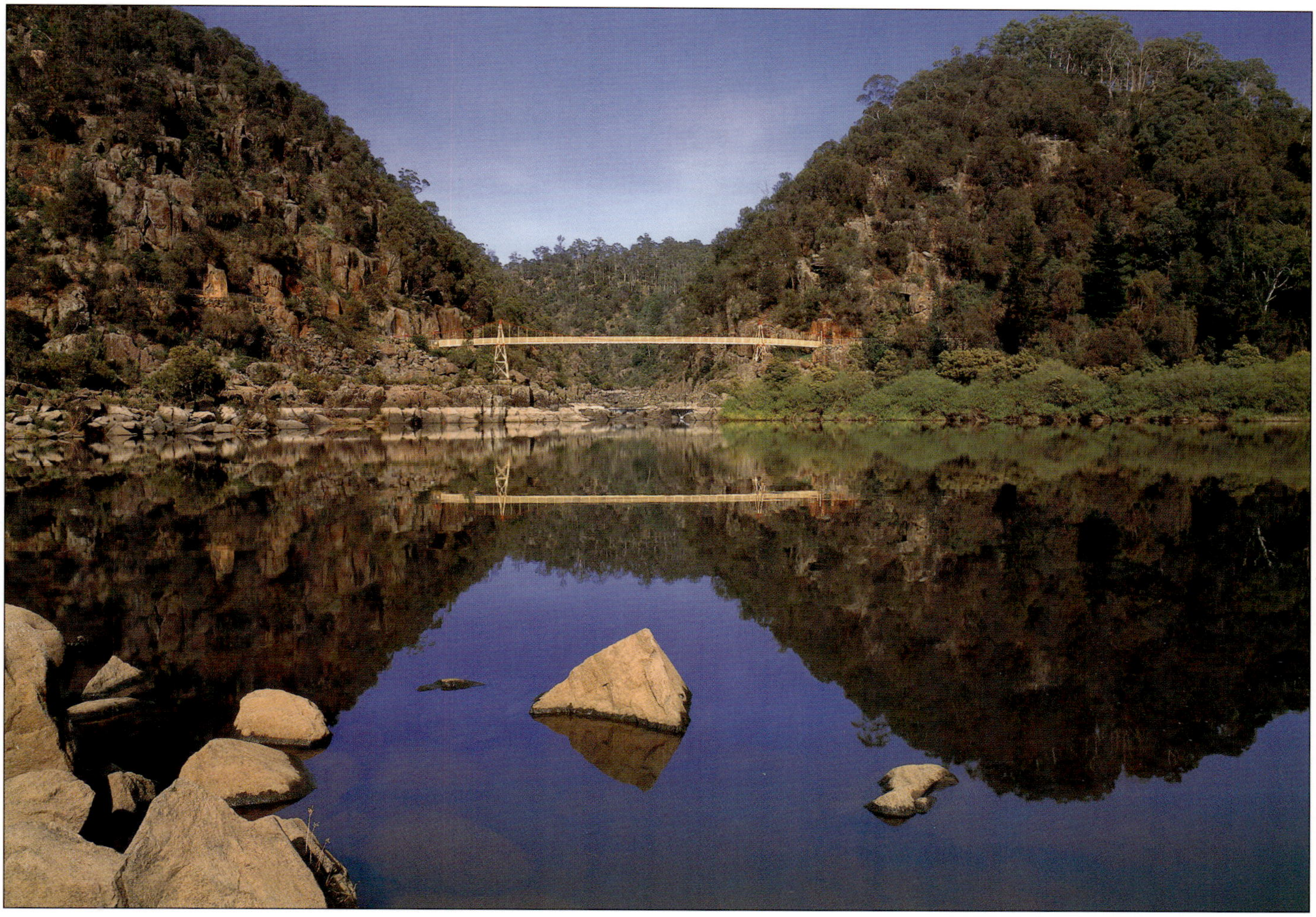

First Basin and Alexandra Suspension Bridge, Cataract Gorge Reserve, Launceston.

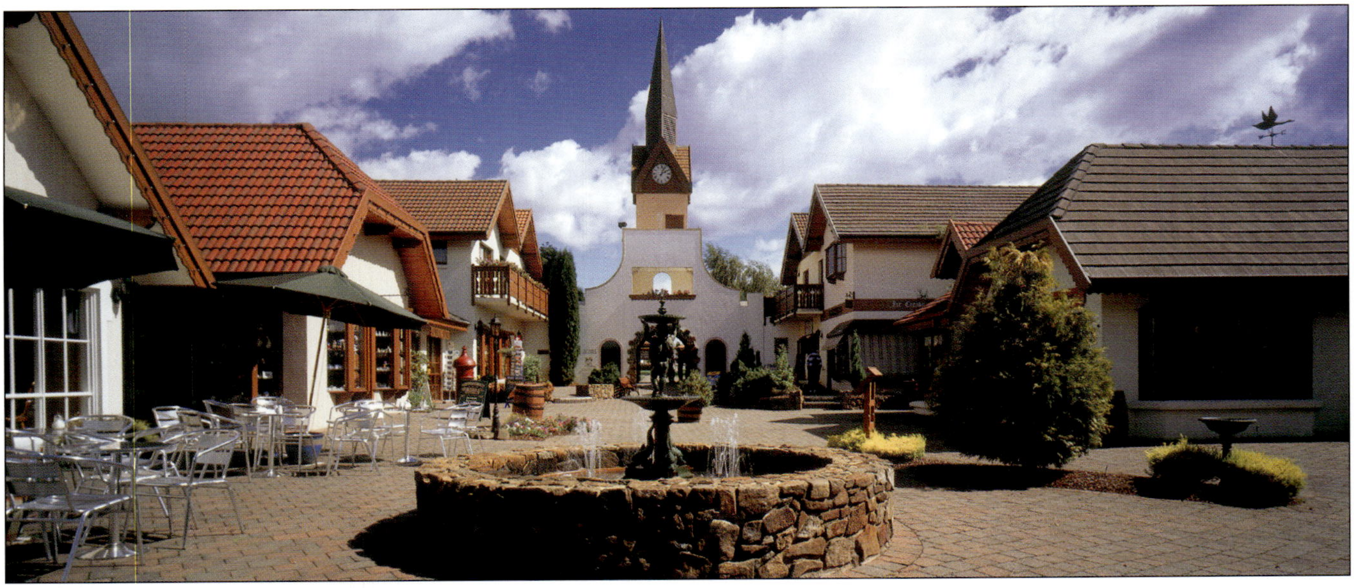

In the picturesque Tamar Valley, Grindelwald captures the essence of a traditional Swiss Village.

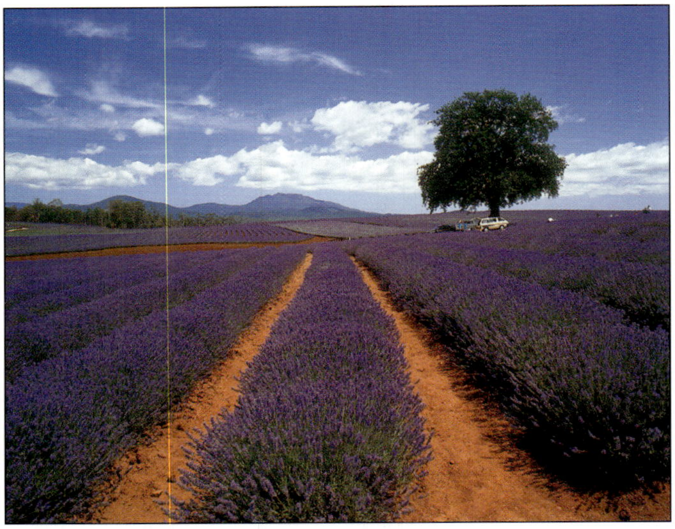

Bridestowe Estate Lavender Farm, Nabowla.

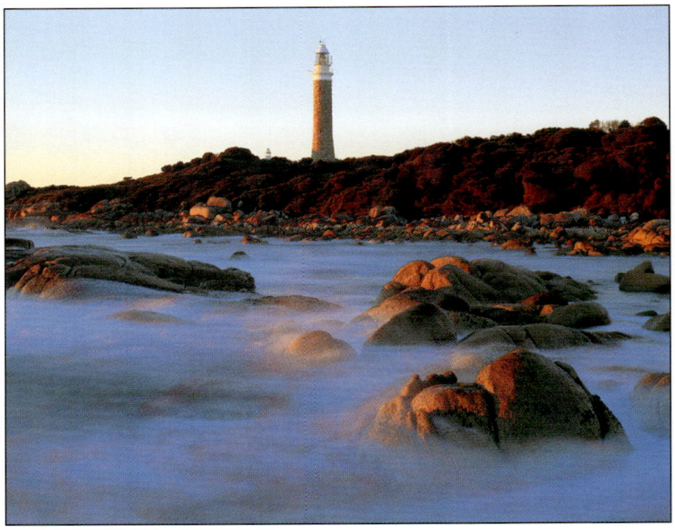

Dawn at Eddystone Point.

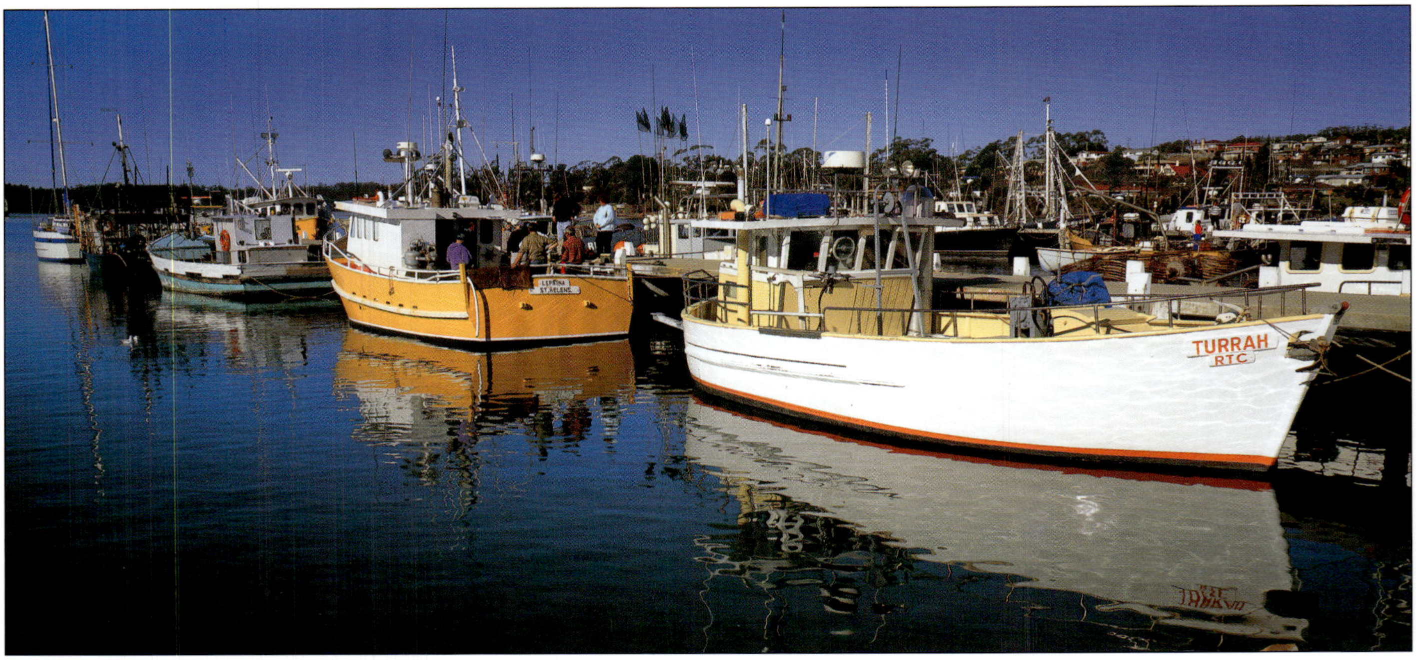

Fishing boats at Refit Wharf, Georges Bay, St Helens.

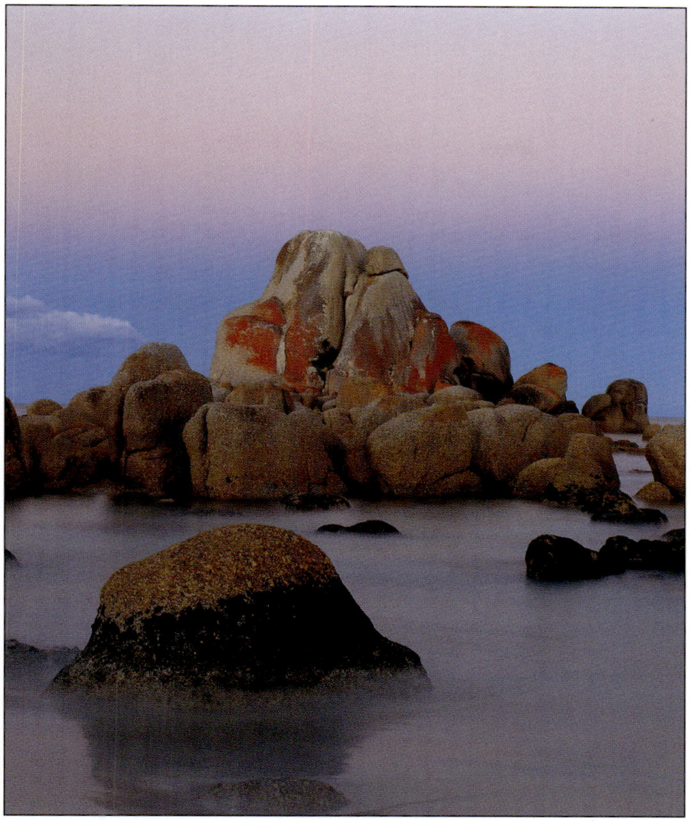

Afterglow at Picnic Rocks, Mount William National Park.

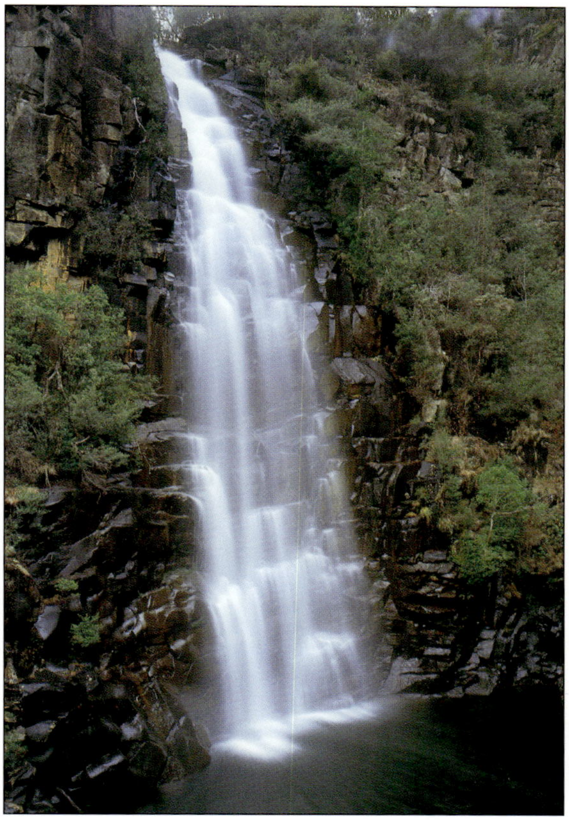

Meetus Falls.

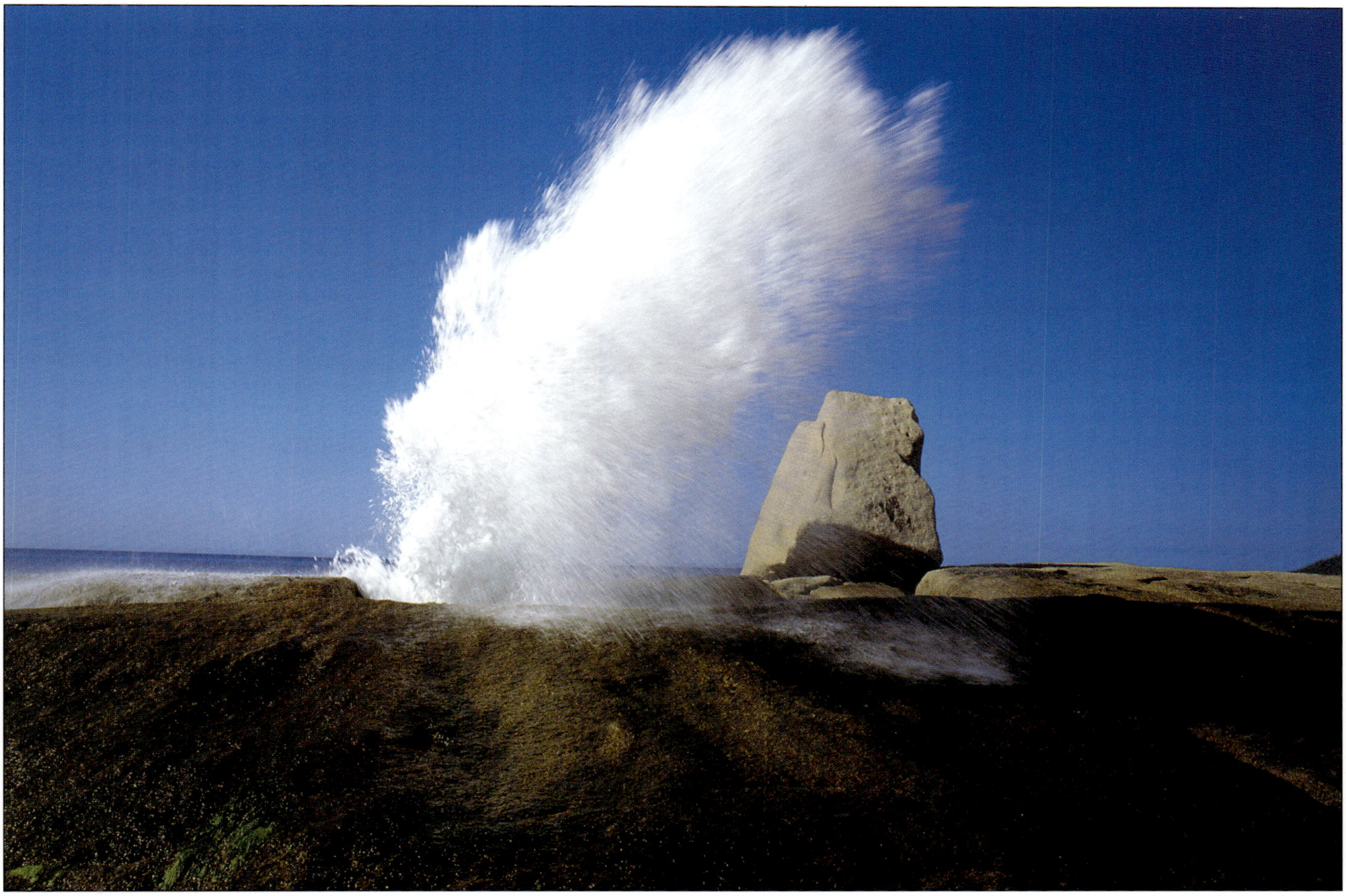

The Blowhole, Bicheno.

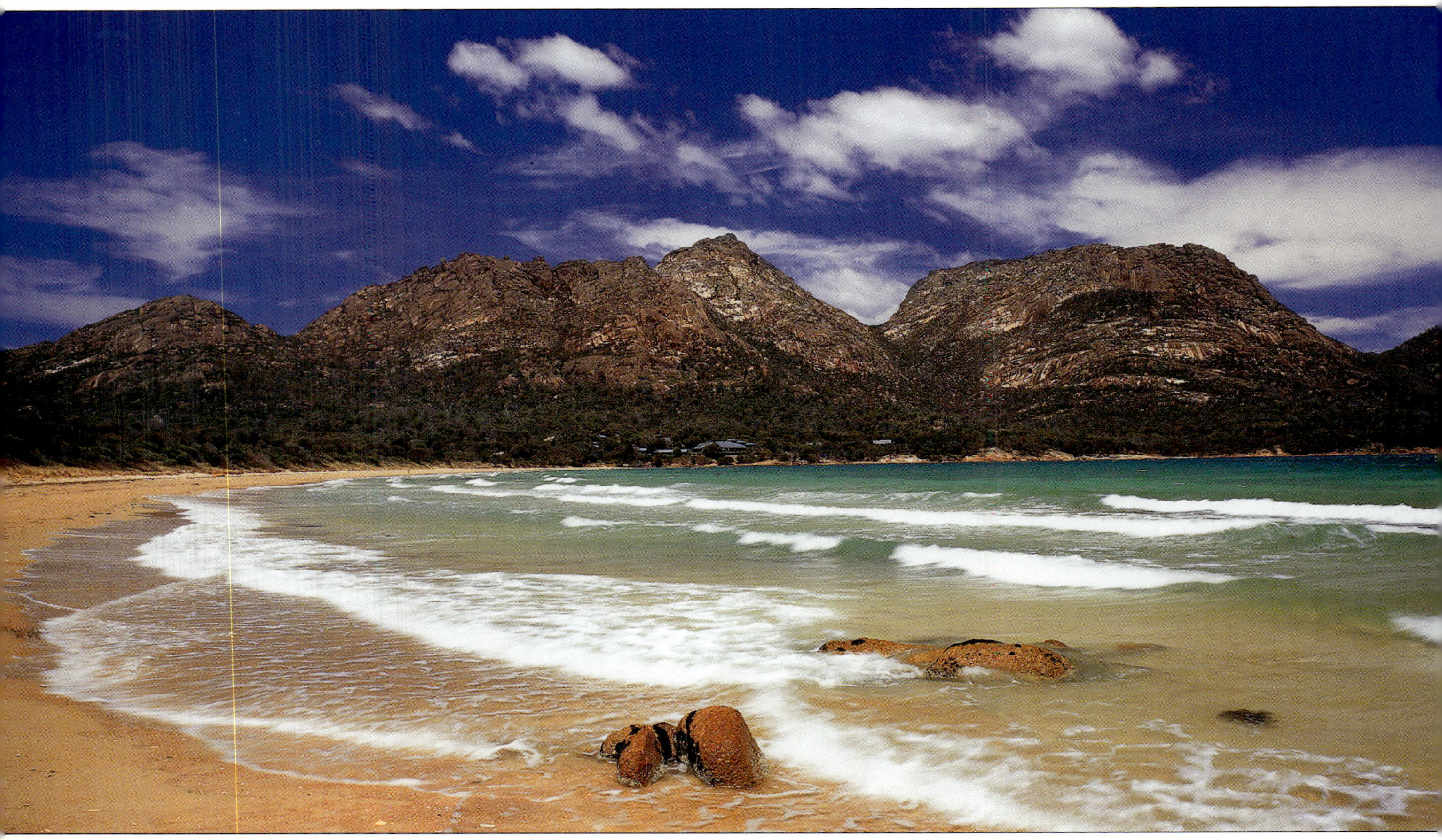

The Hazards from Richardsons Beach, Coles Bay.

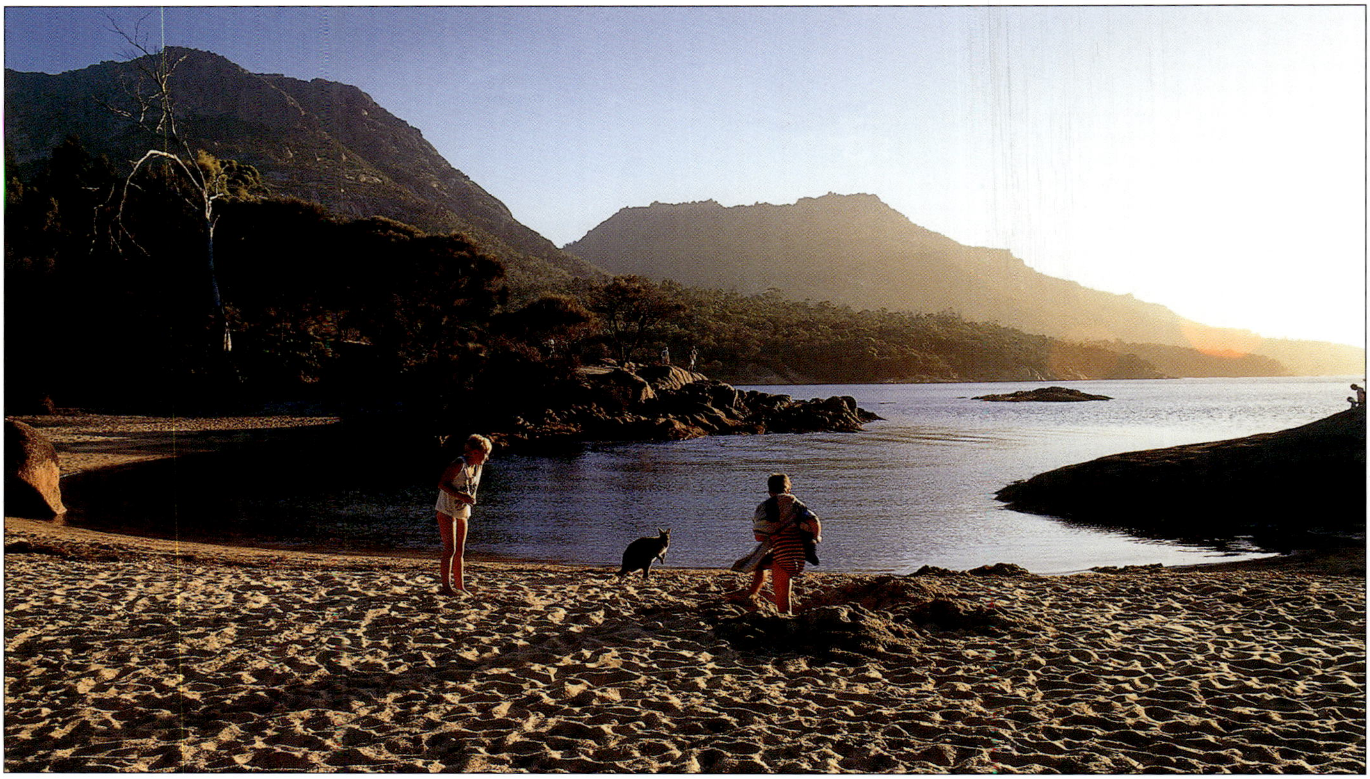

The beautiful calm of Honeymoon Bay.

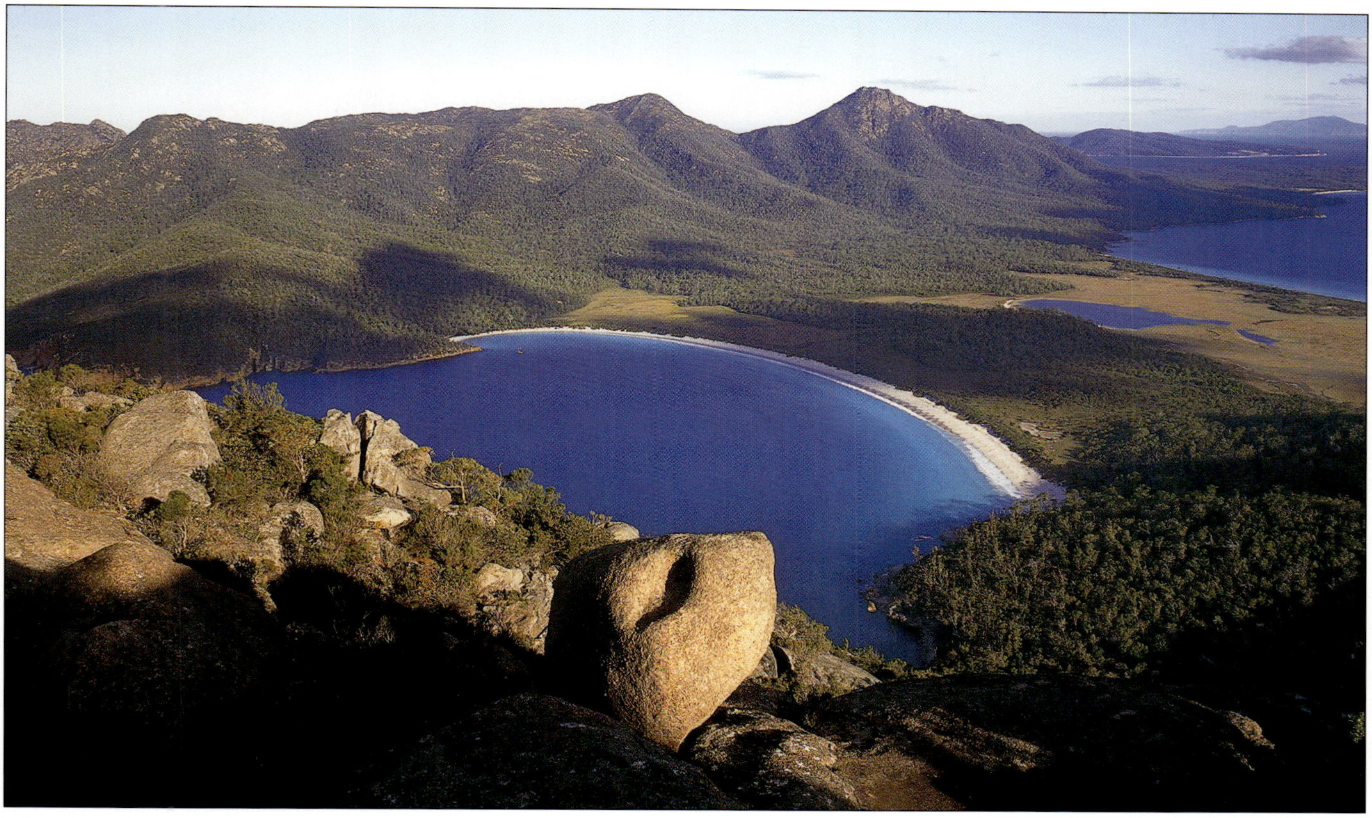

Wineglass Bay from the summit of Mount Amos.

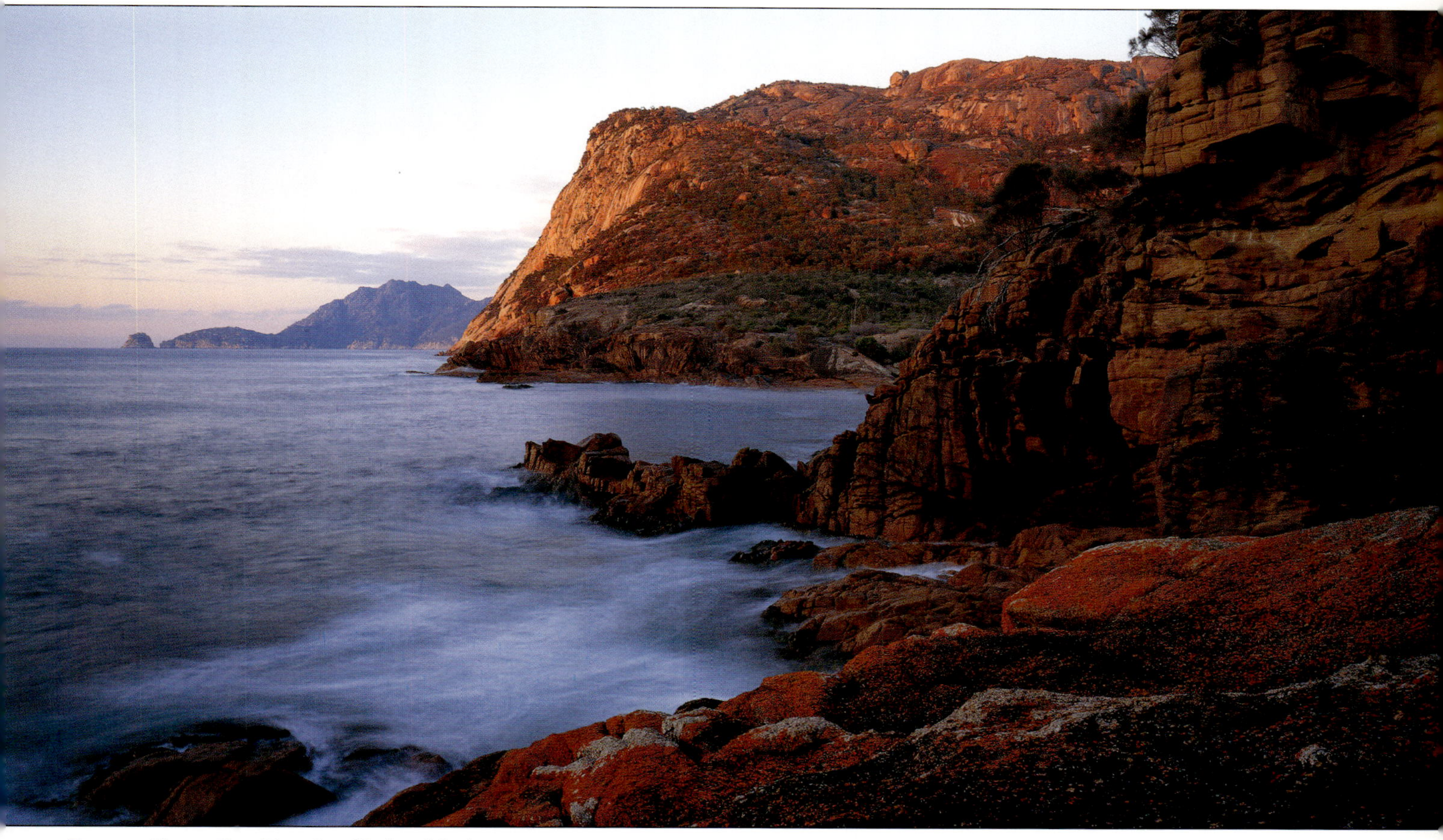

Dawn at Sleepy Bay, Freycinet National Park.

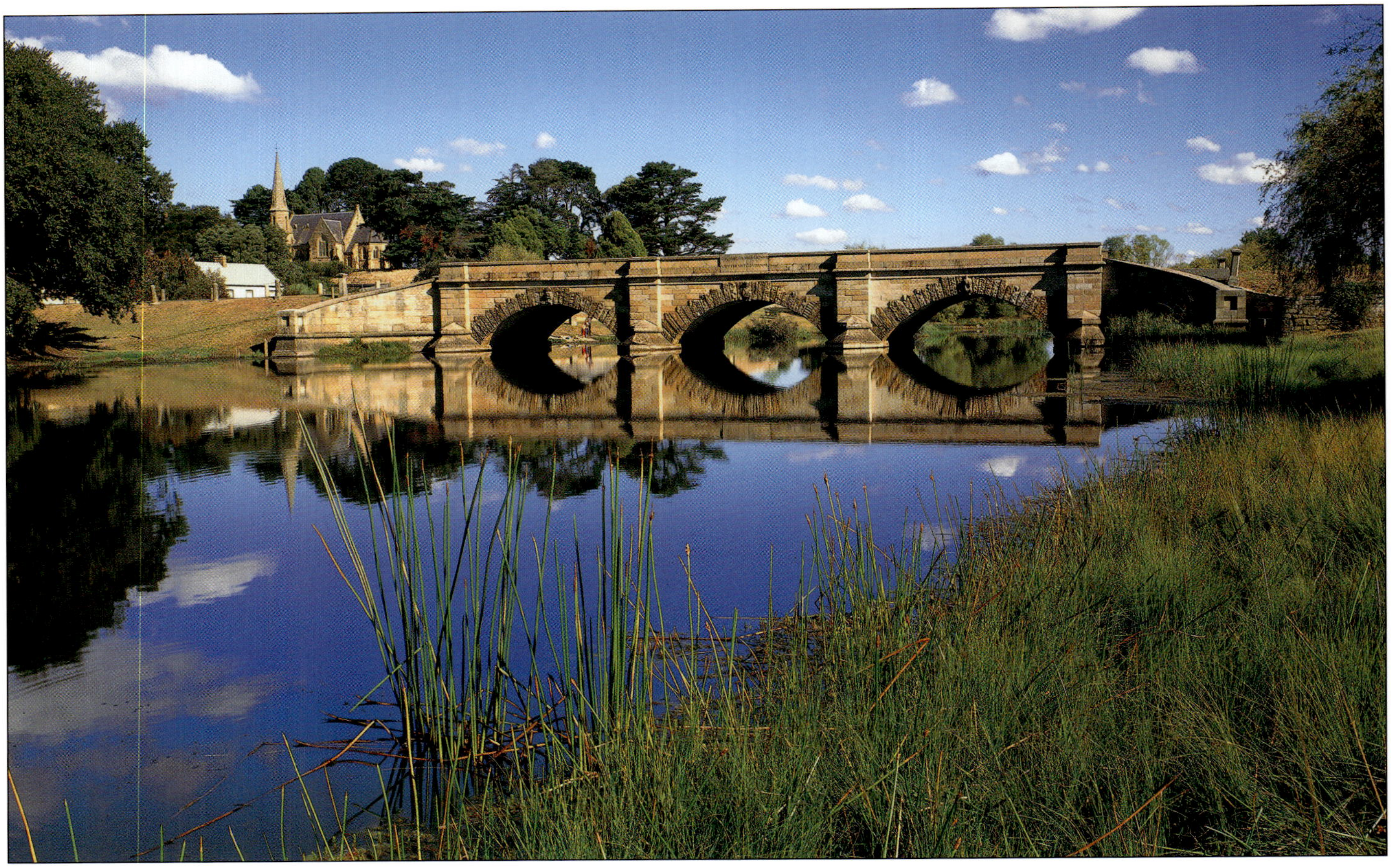

Ross Bridge (1836) reflects in the Macquarie River.

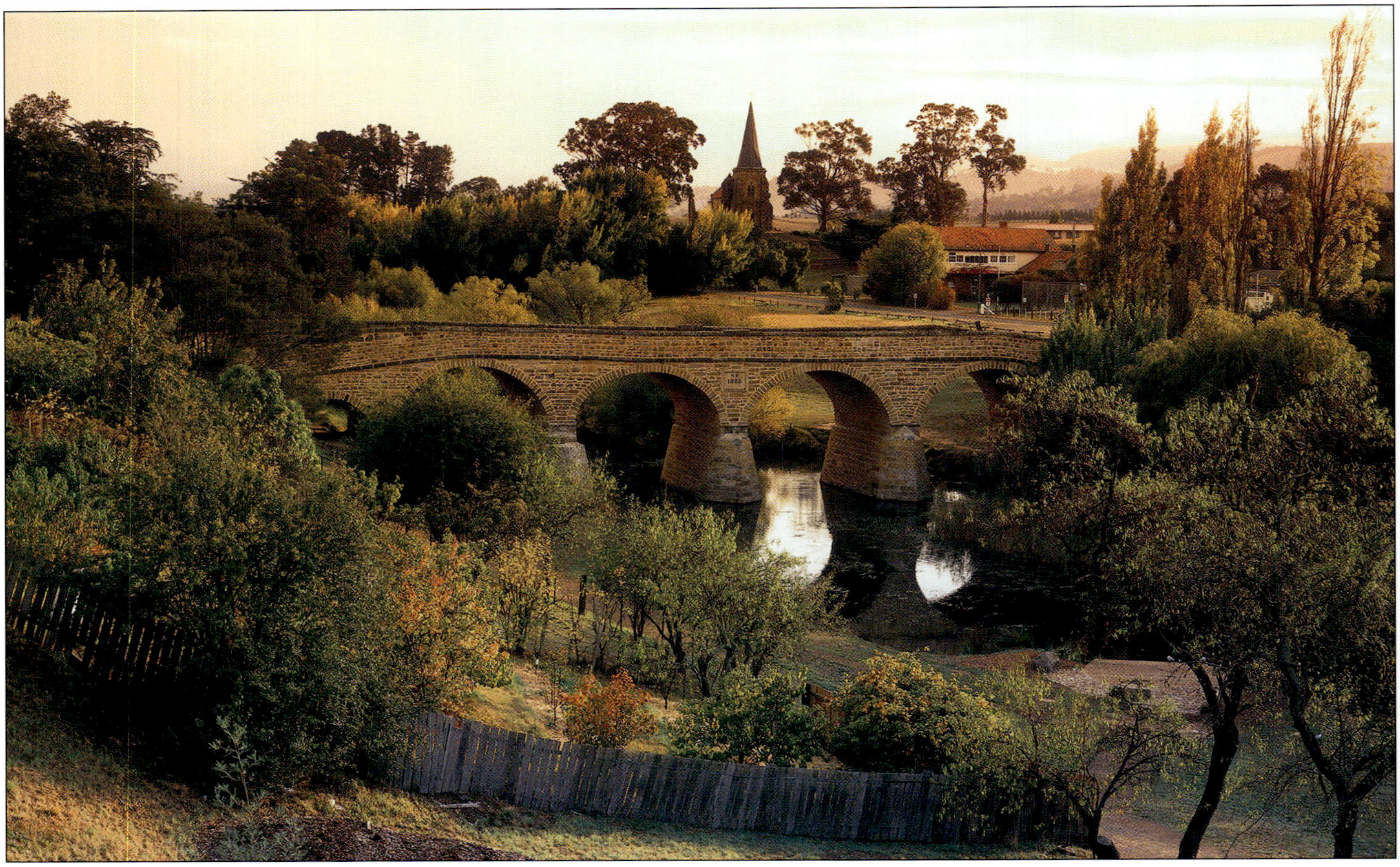

Built by convict labour in 1823, Richmond Bridge is Australia's oldest stone bridge.

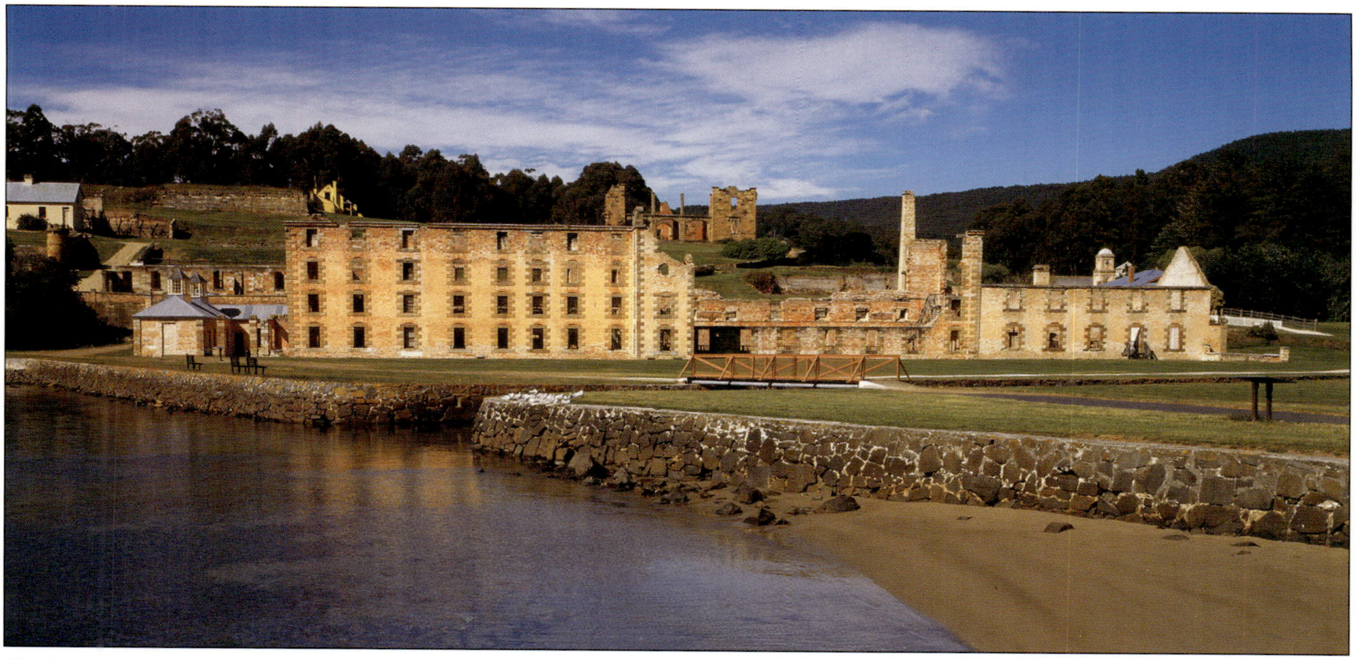

The Penitentiary is the largest building at Port Arthur and could house up to 484 convicts.

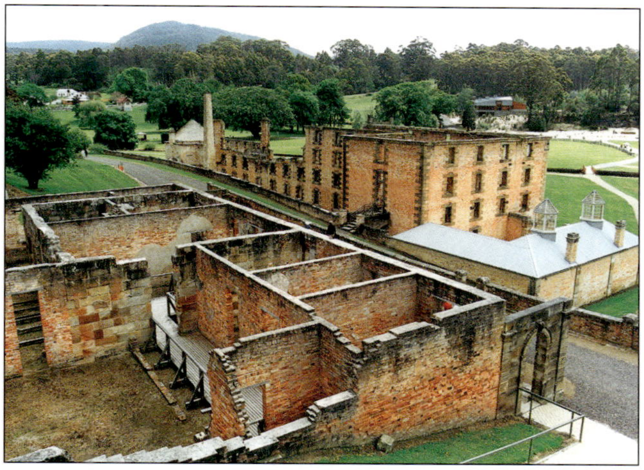

The Commandant's Offices and The Penitentiary.

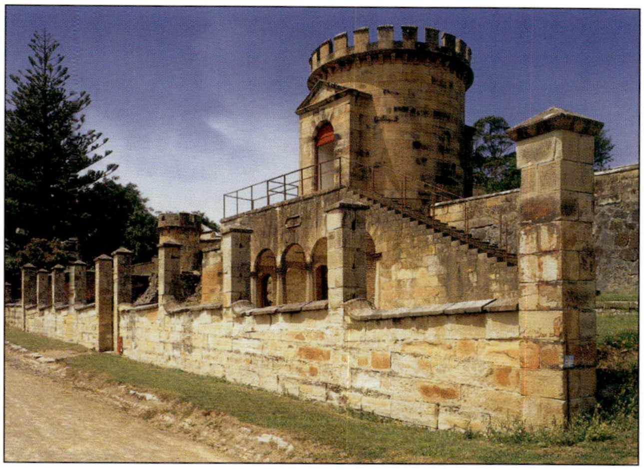

The circular Guard Tower.

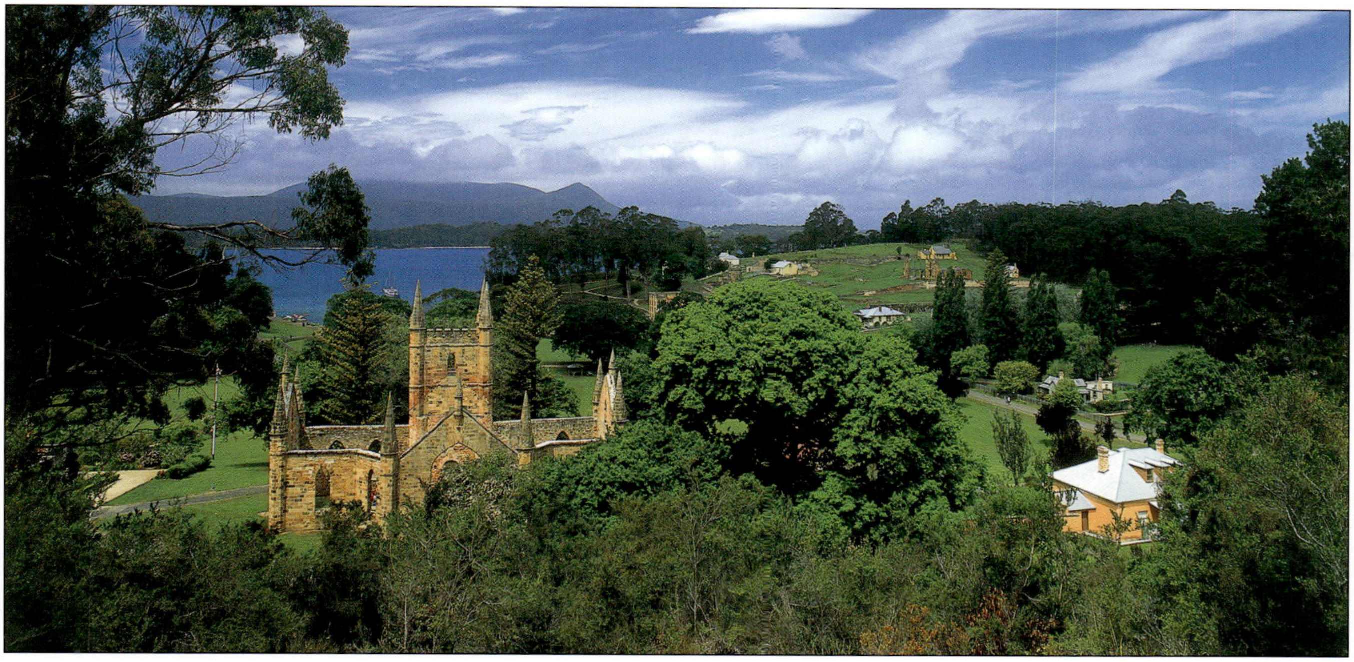

Port Arthur from Scorpion Rock, today's peaceful scene hides the brutality of the past.

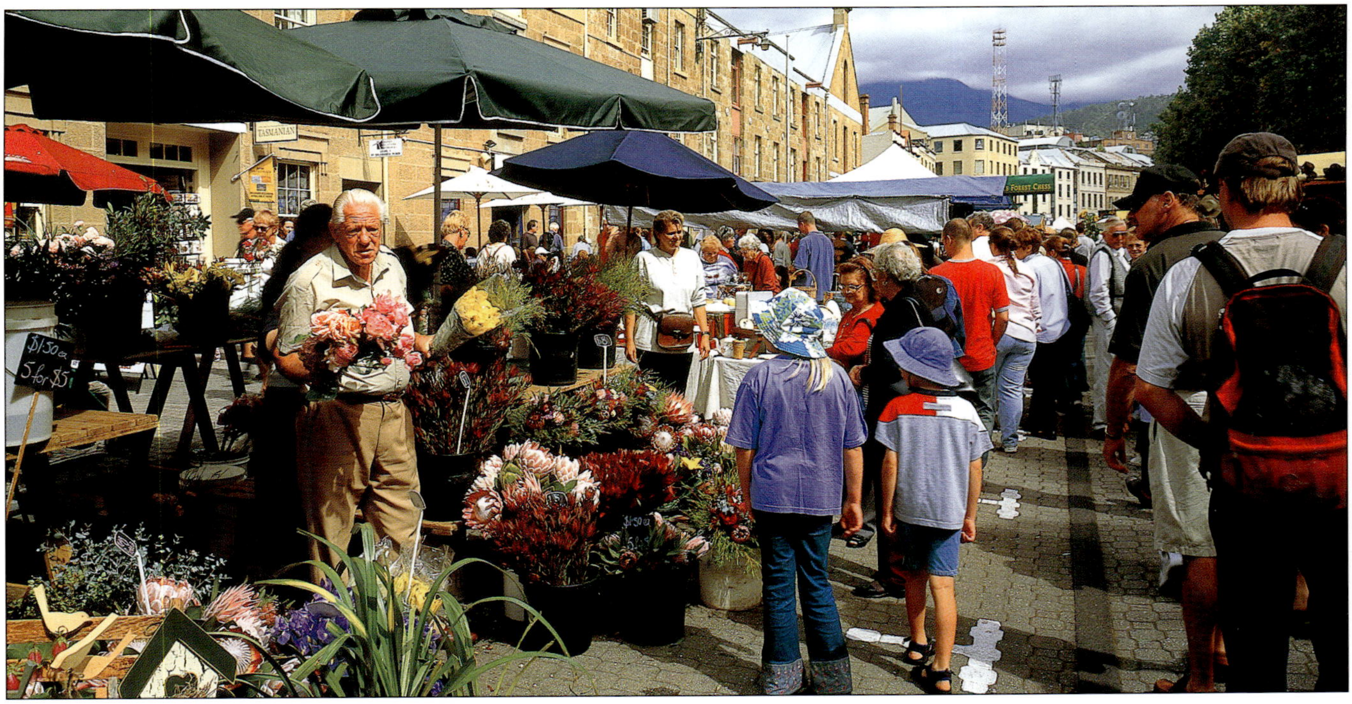

Salamanca market, a colourful open-air market held every Saturday.

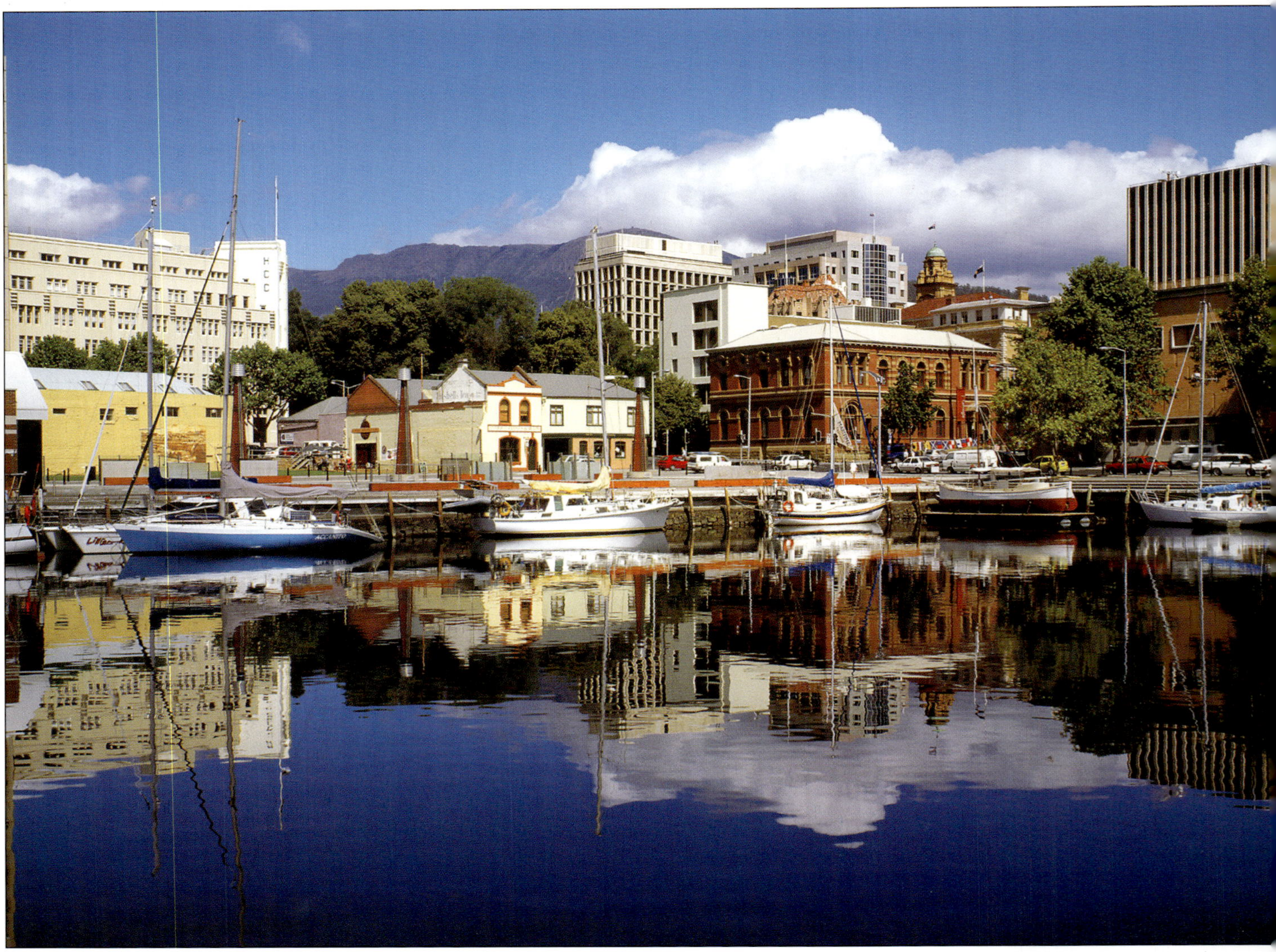

Constitution Dock, Hobart.

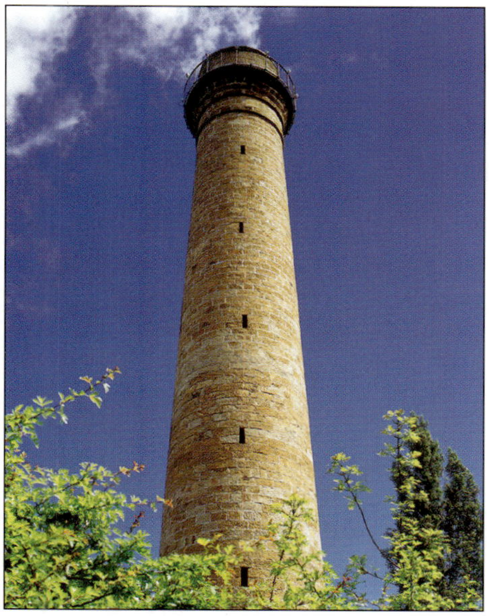

The Shot Tower, Taroona.

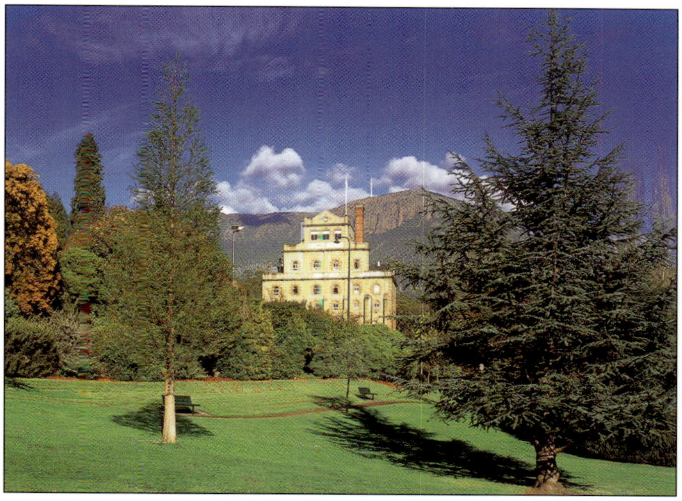

Cascade Brewery, Australia's oldest brewery.

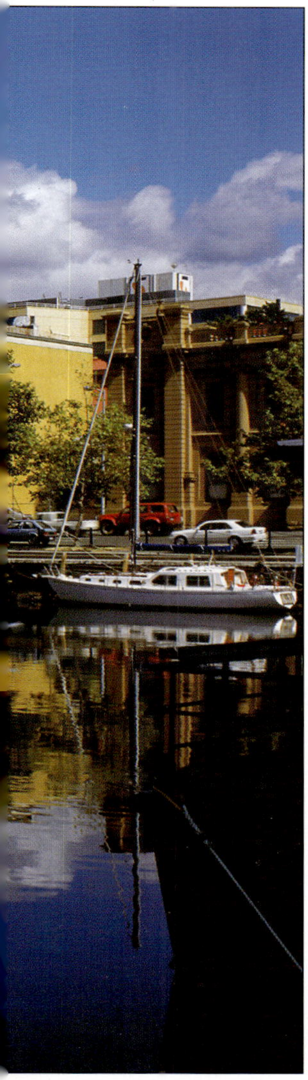

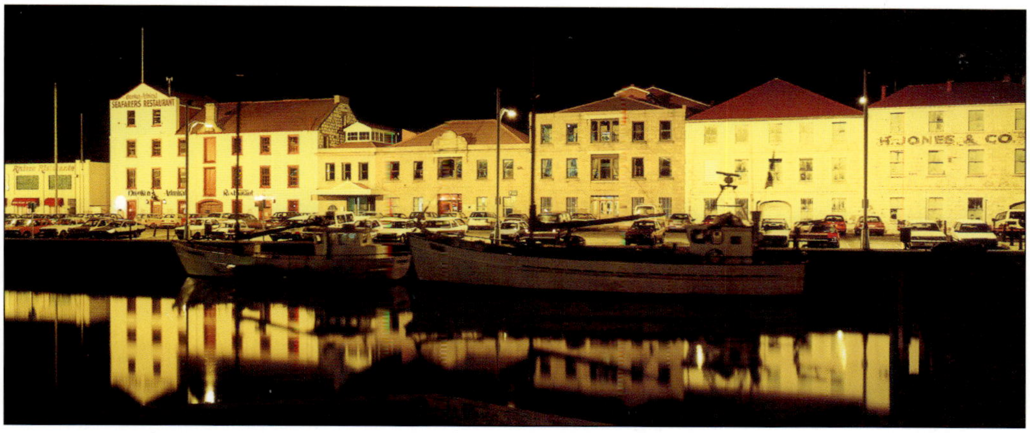

Sandstone warehouses reflect in the placid waters of Victoria Dock.

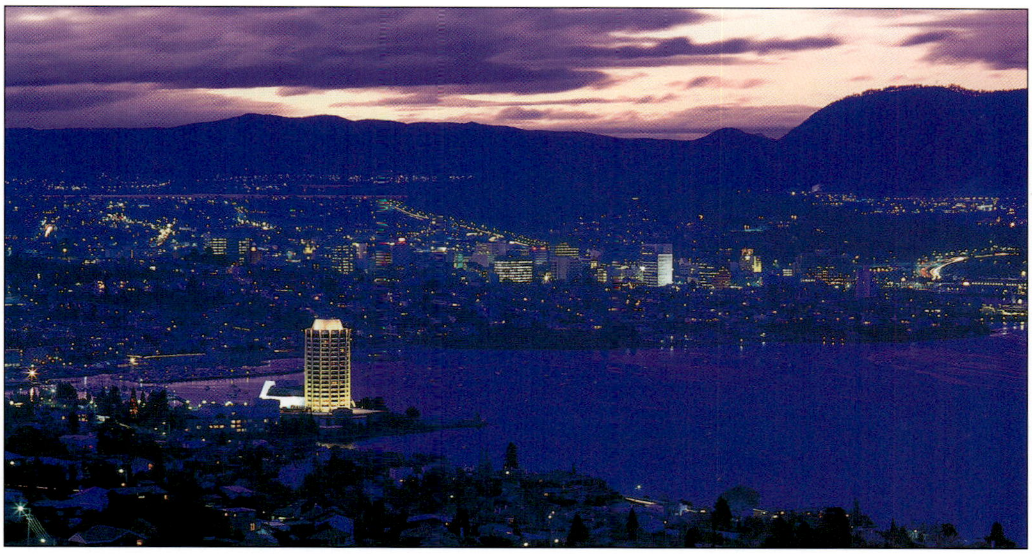

Purple shades of dusk across Hobart and its harbour.

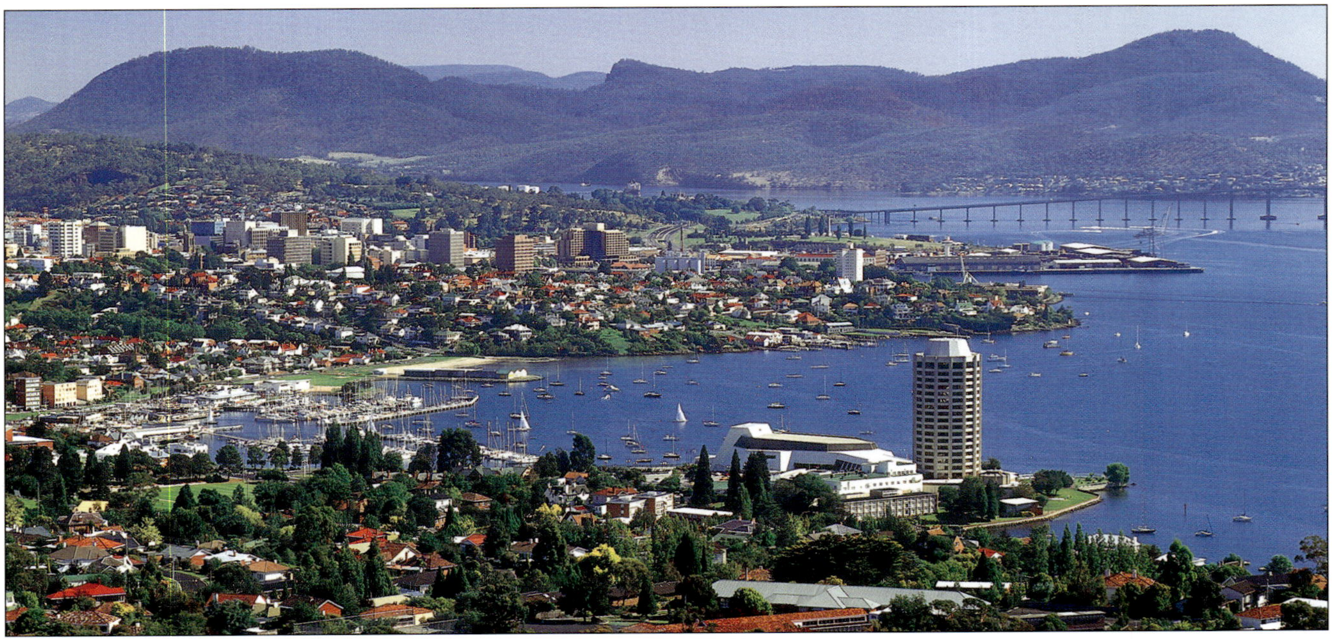

Hobart and the Derwent River from Sandy Bay.

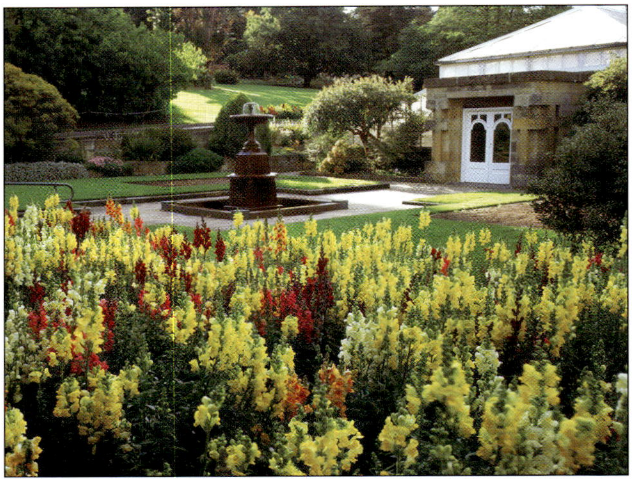

The Royal Tasmanian Botanical Gardens.

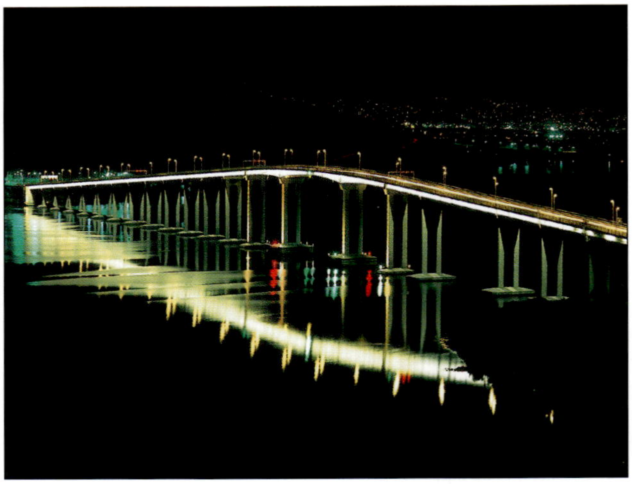

The Tasman Bridge from Rosny Hill.

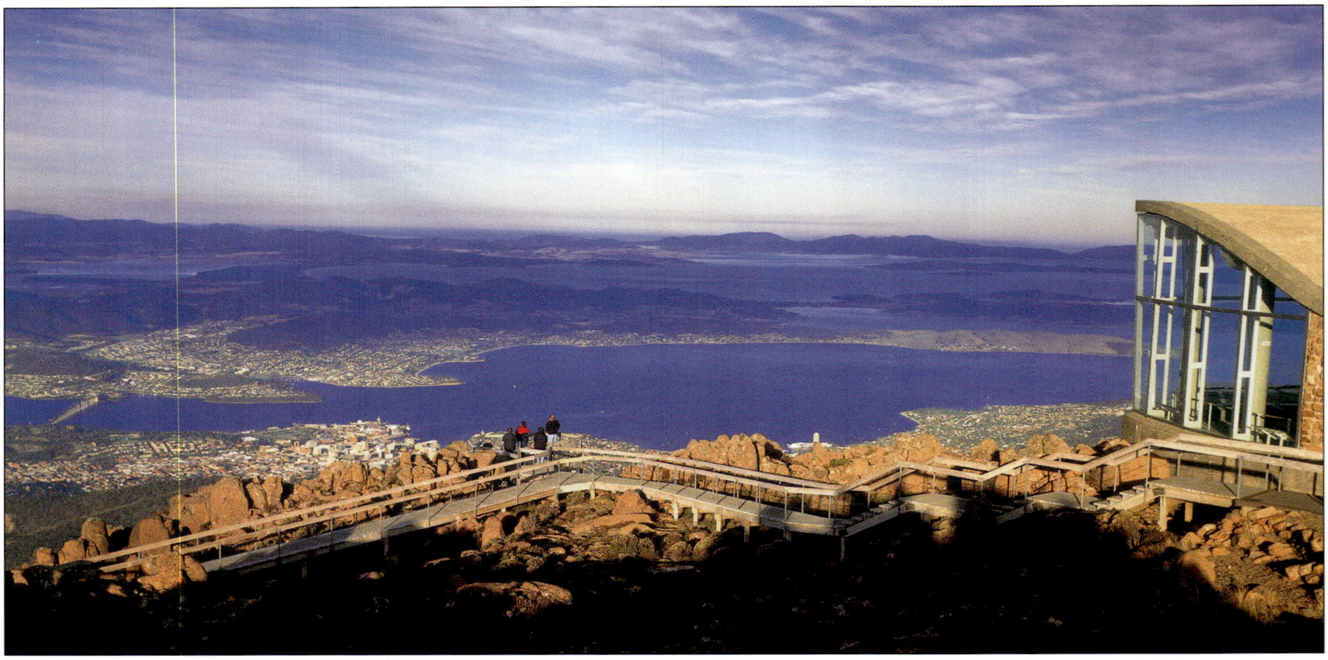

Spectacular view of Hobart from the summit of Mount Wellington.

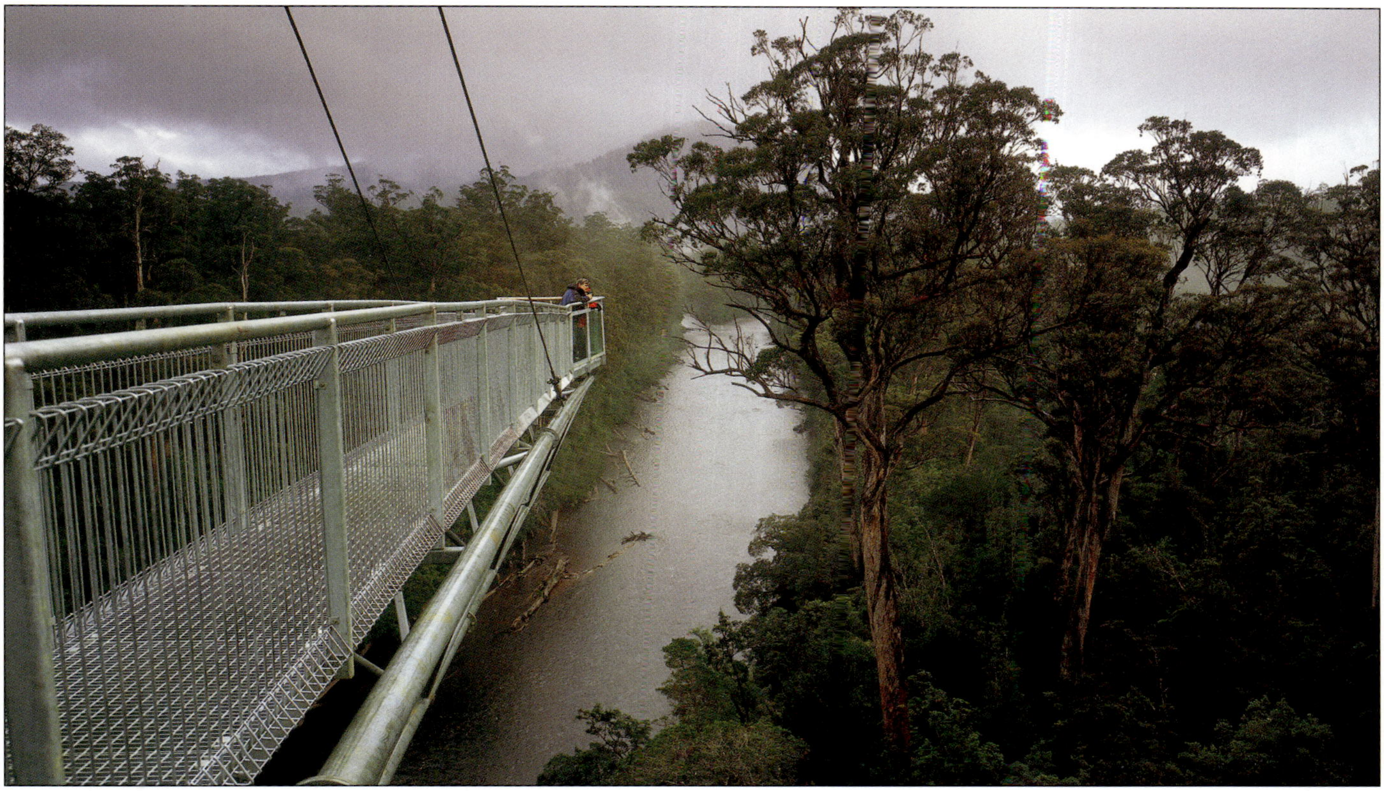

Stunning treetop views 37 metres above the Huon River, Tahune Forest Air Walk.

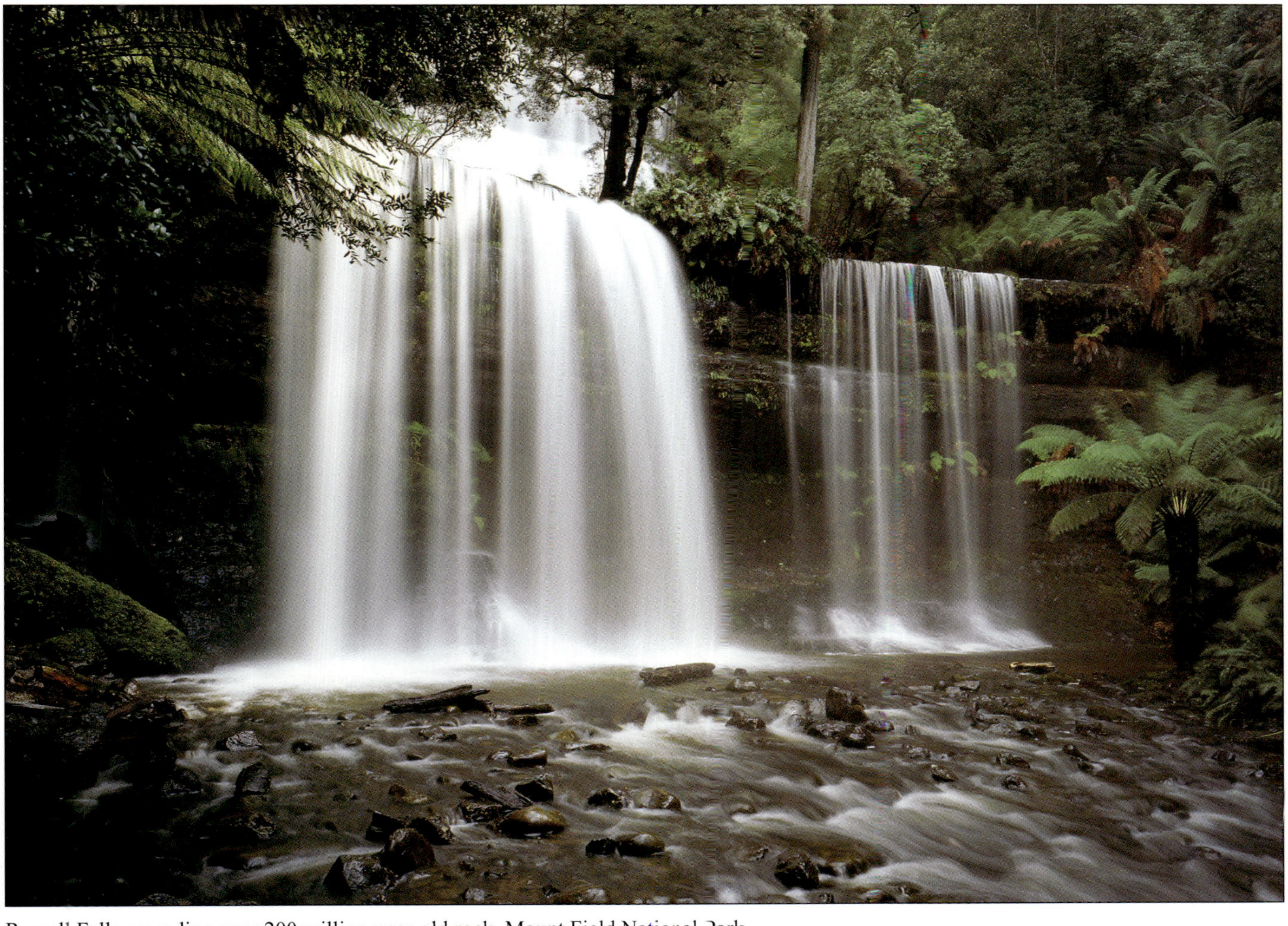

Russell Falls cascading over 200 million-year-old rock, Mount Field National Park.

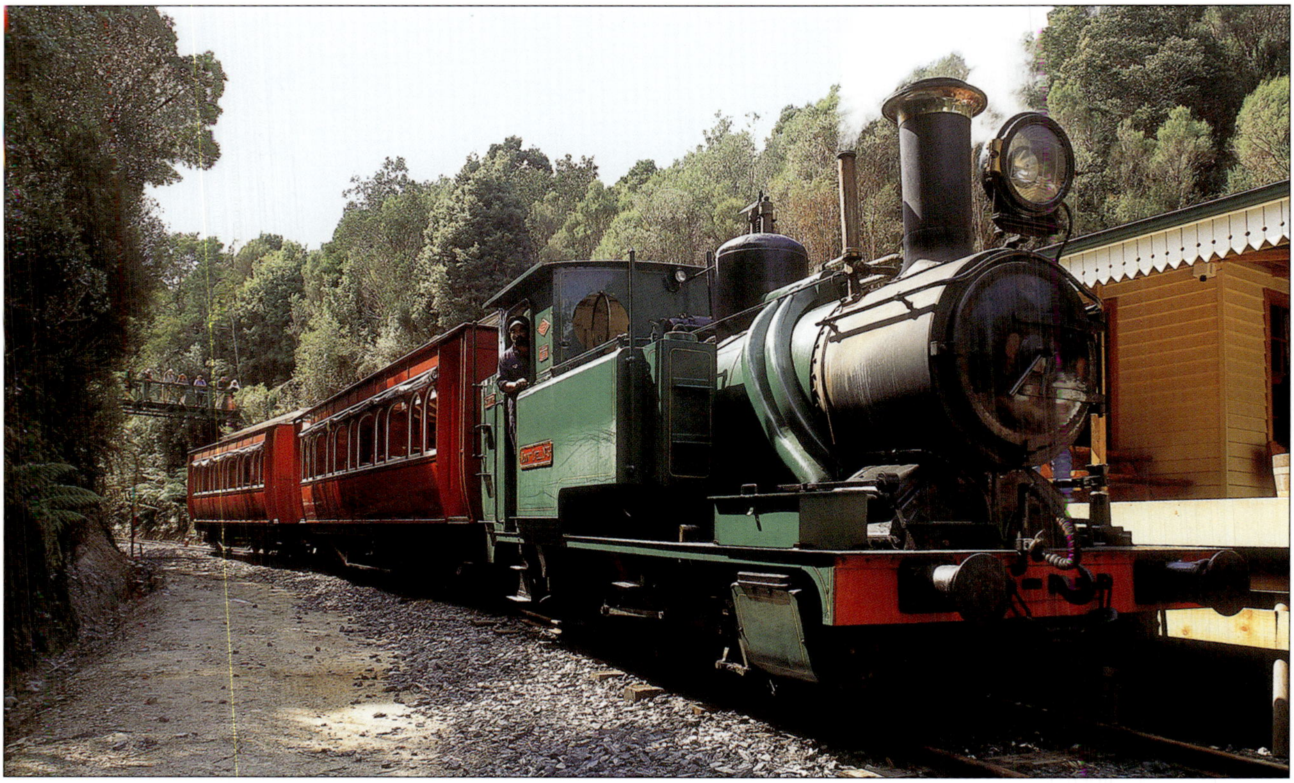

West Coast Wilderness Railway, Australia's only rack and pinion railway.

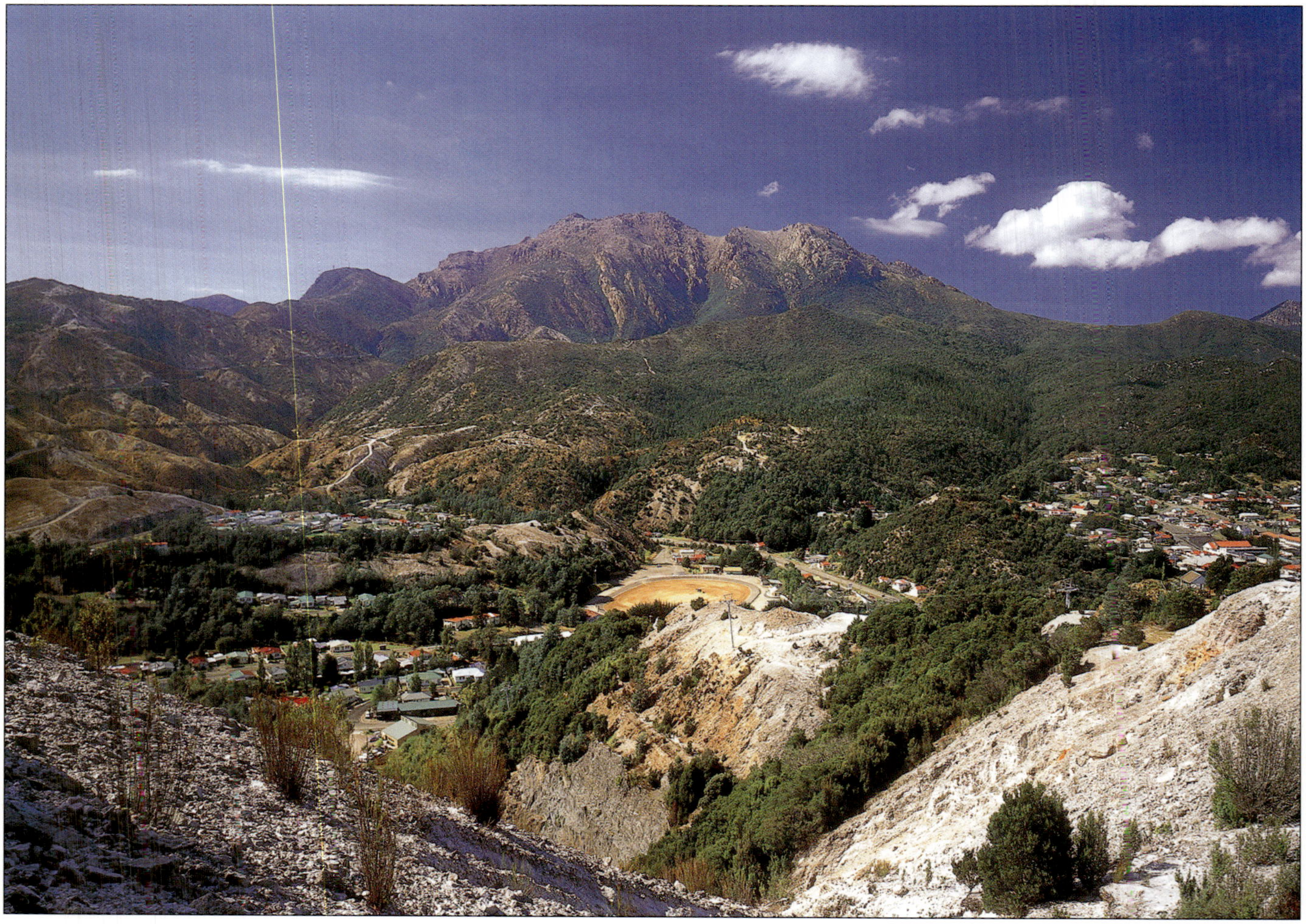

Vegetation slowly reclaims the hills of Queenstown.

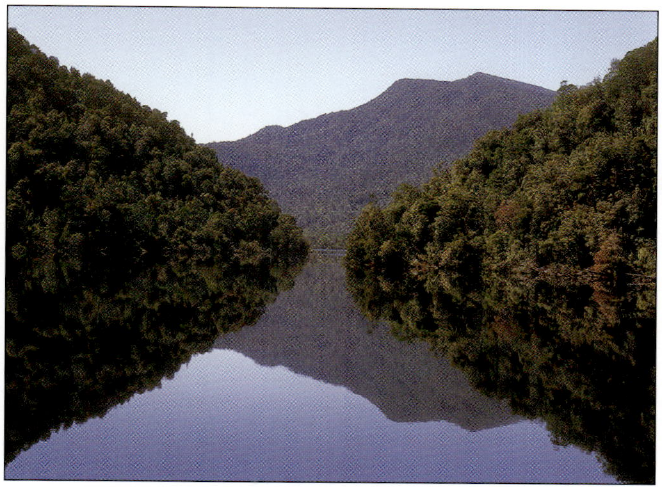

Mirrored reflections in the Gordon River.

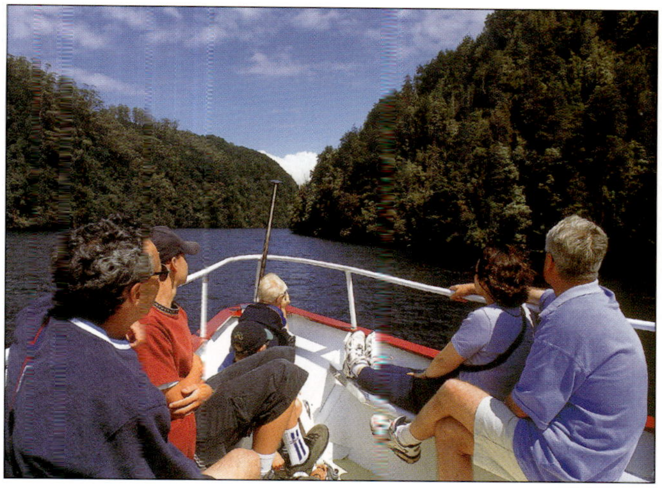

The Gordon River Cruise.

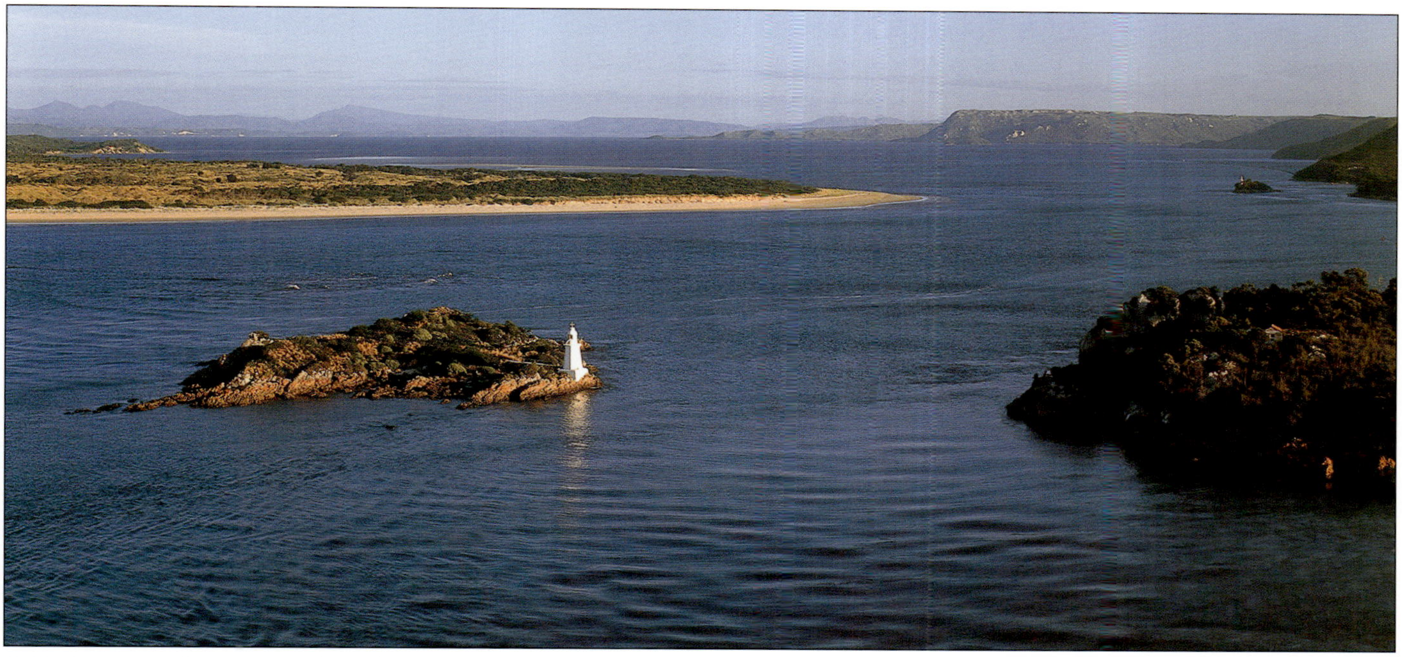

Hell's Gates, notorious entrance from the sea to Macquarie Harbour.

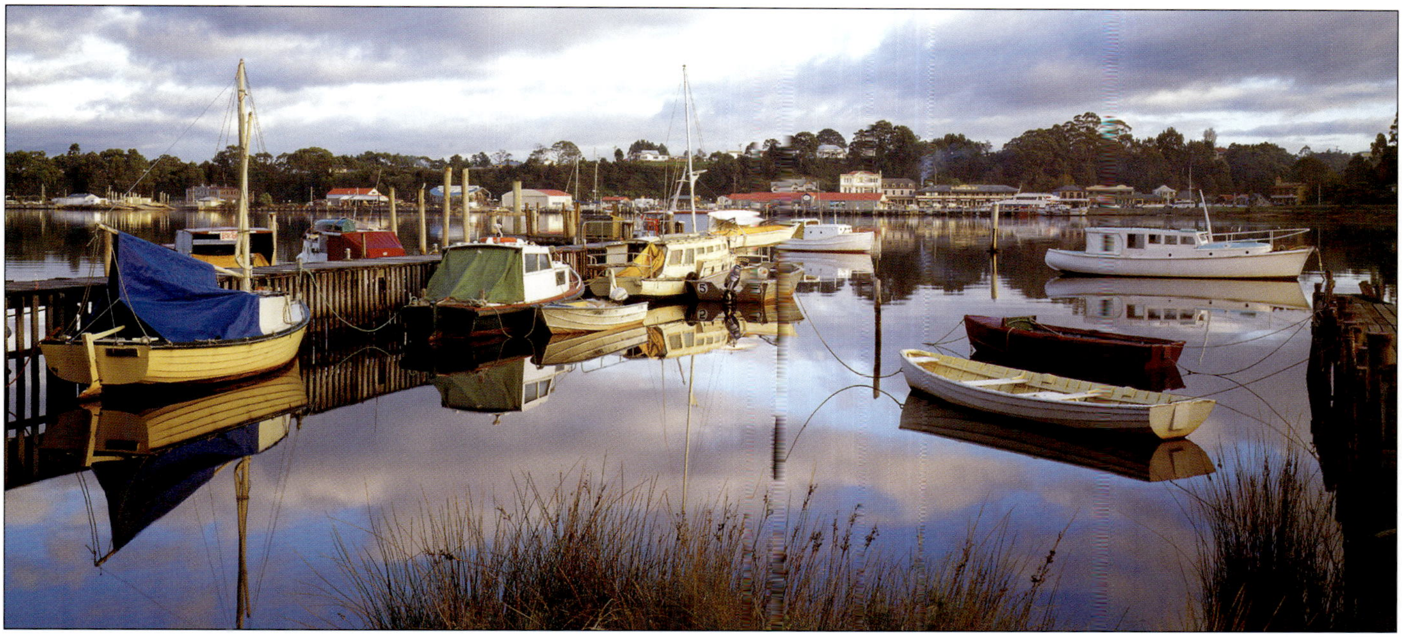

Strahan Harbour from Risby Cove.

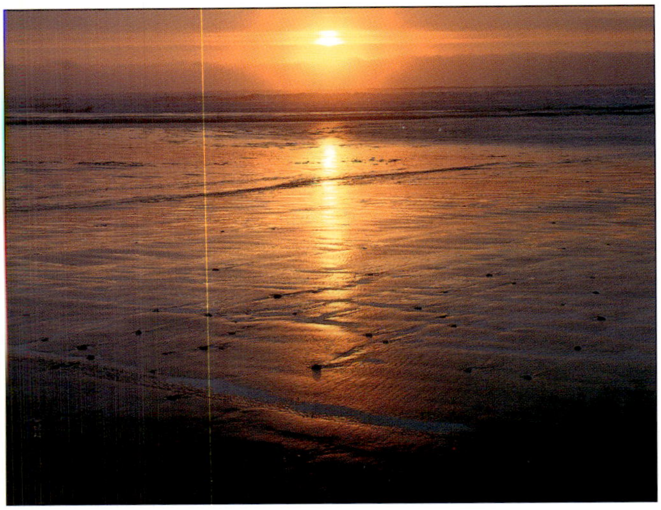

Sunset, Ocean Beach.

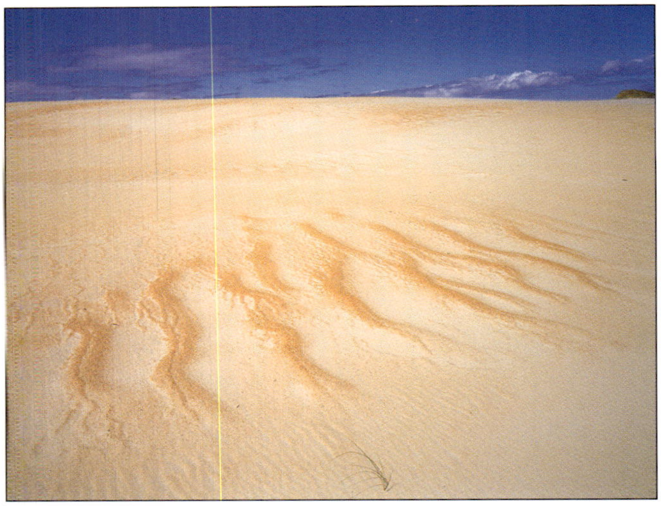

Henty Dunes.

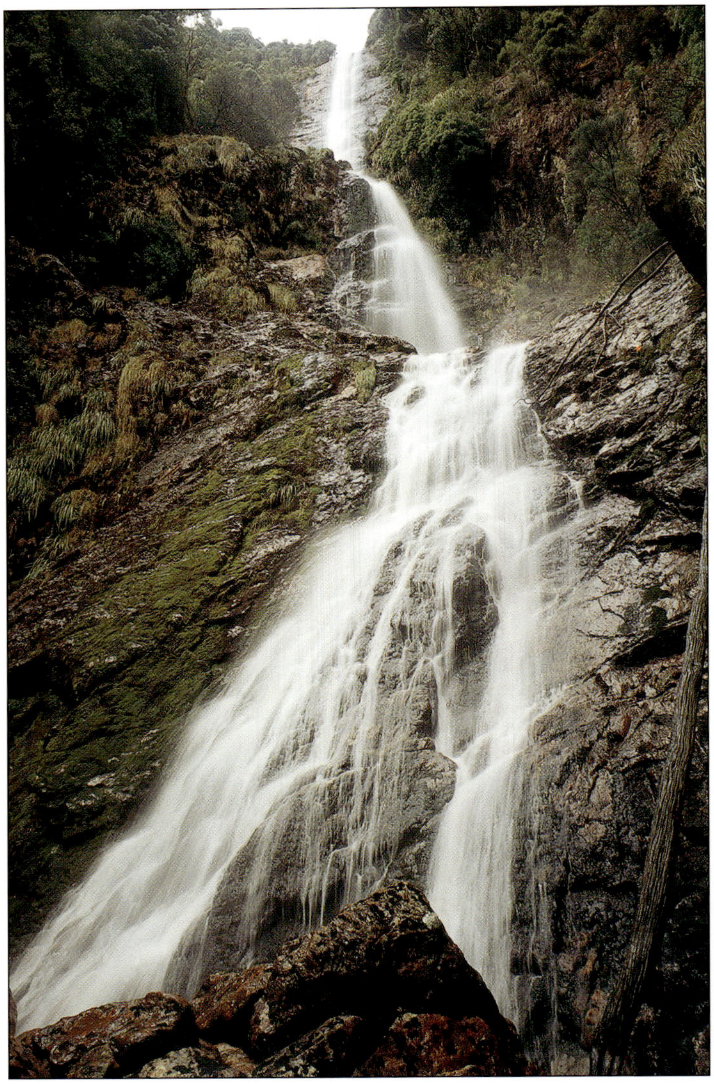

Montezuma Falls, 104 metres high.

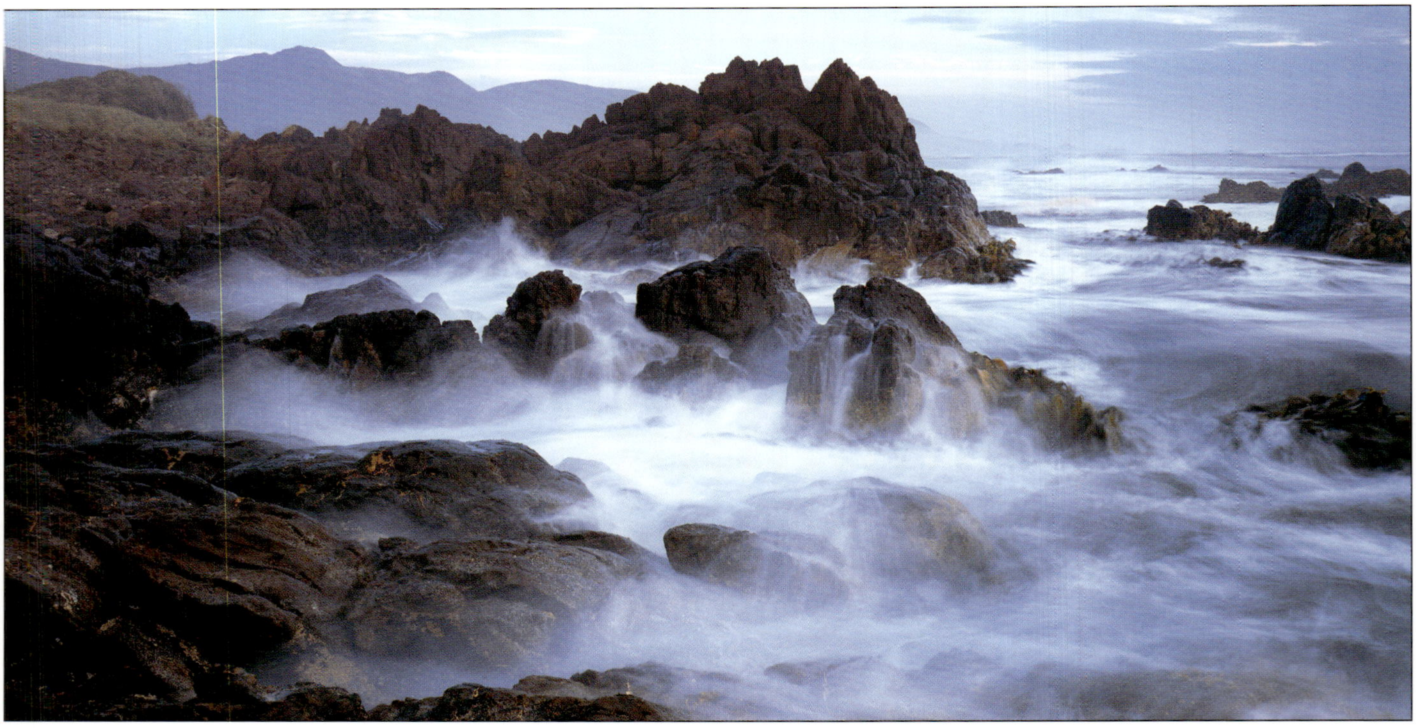

Rugged coastline near Trial Harbour.

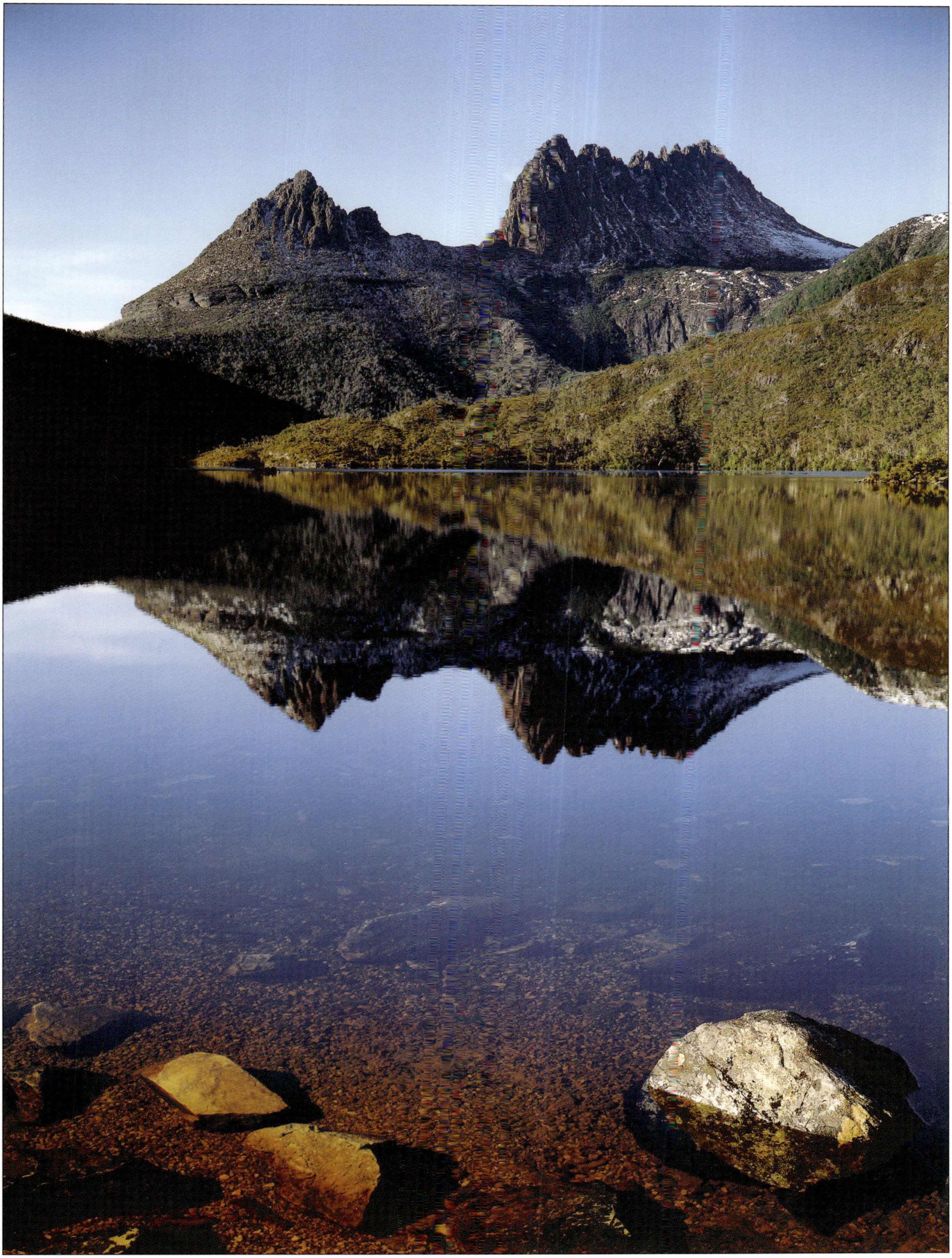

Cradle Mountain from Dove Lake.

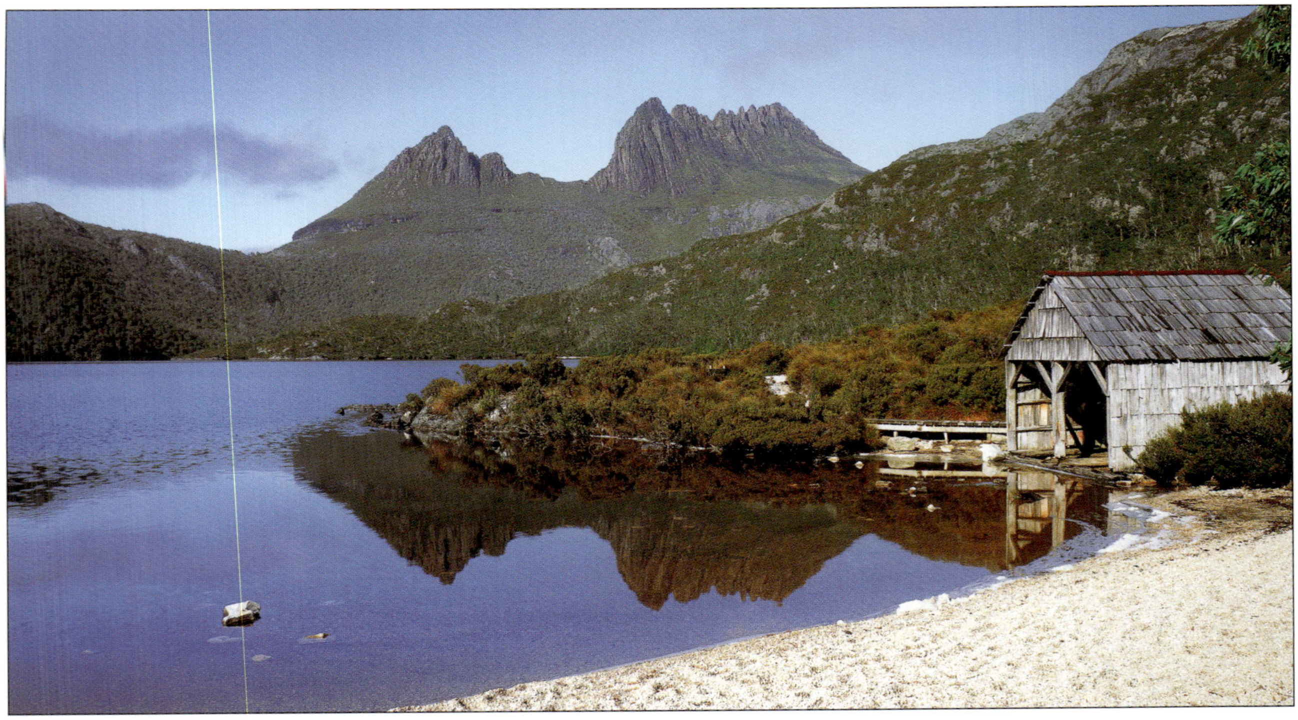

Cradle Mountain and Dove Lake from the Boat Shed.

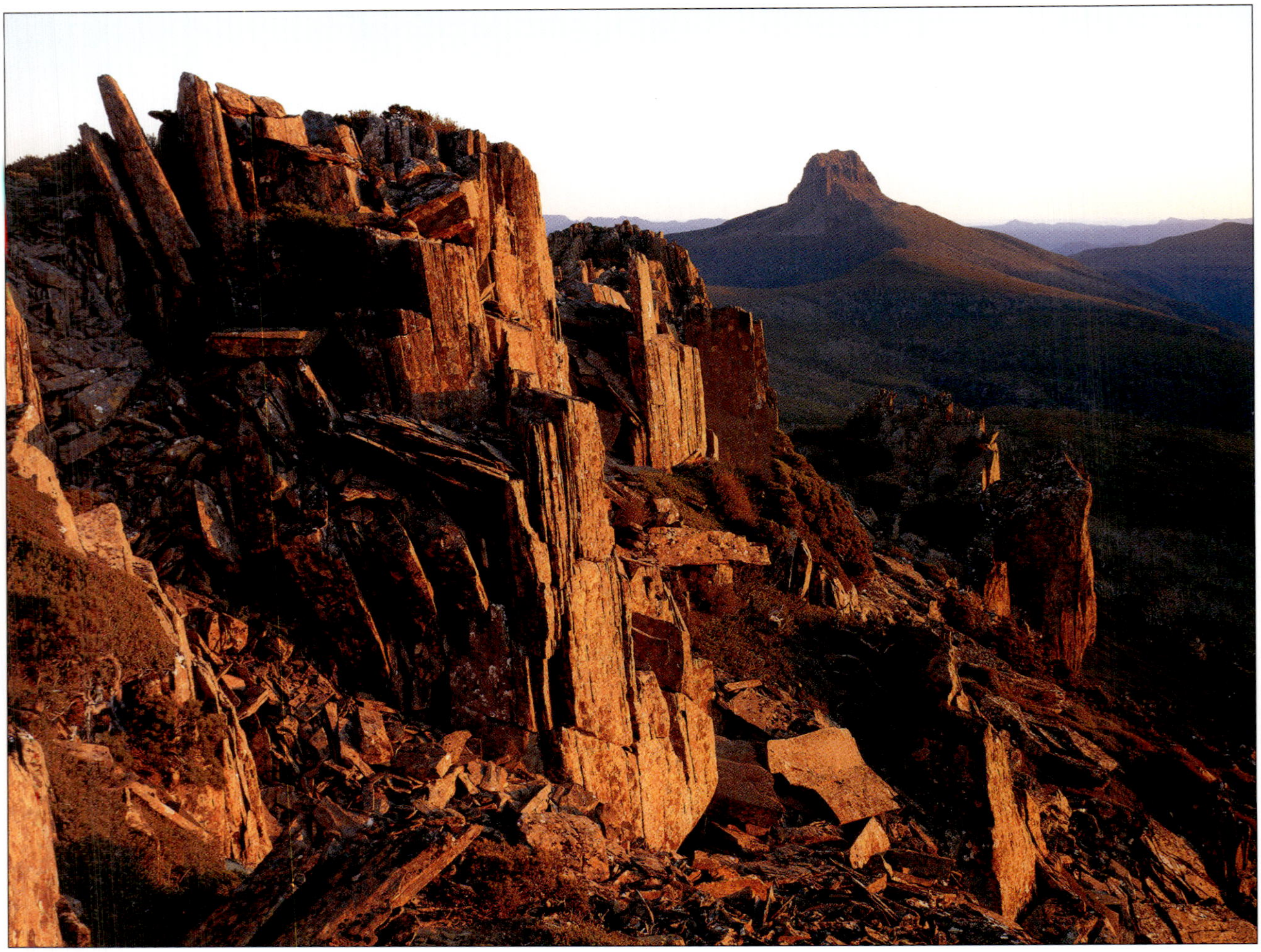

Barn Bluff from Cradle Mountain at sunset.

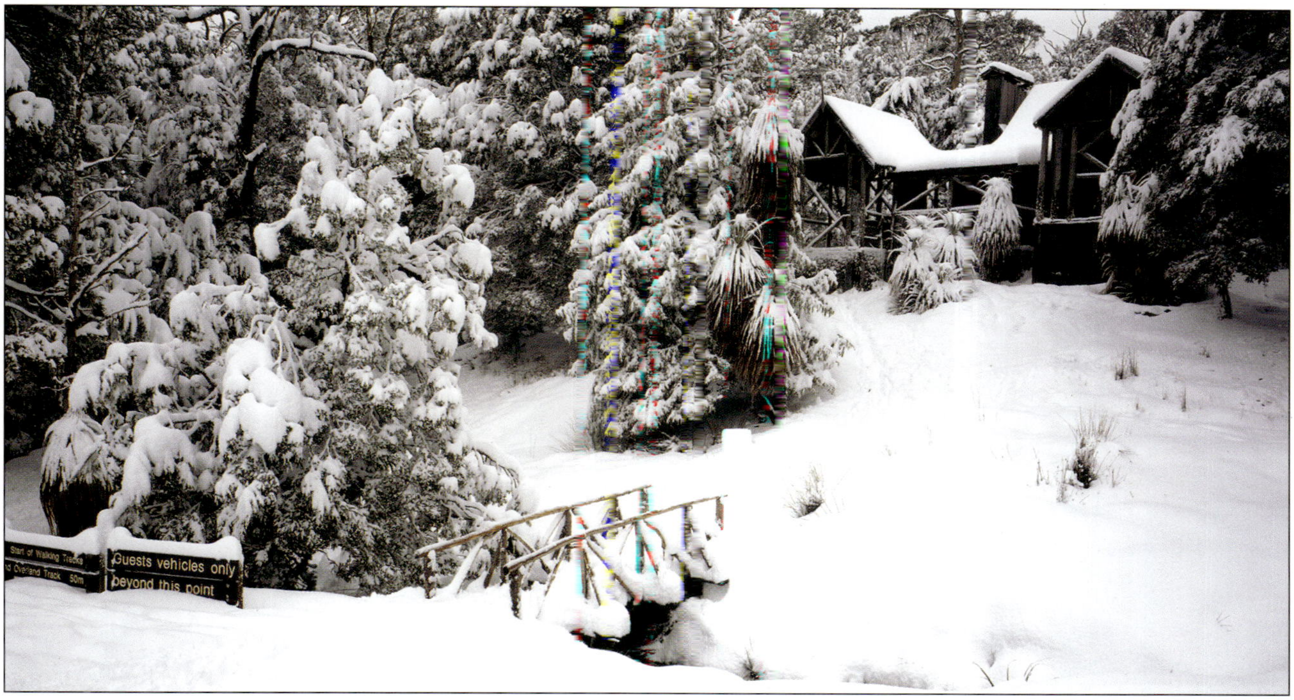

Waldheim Chalet under snow.

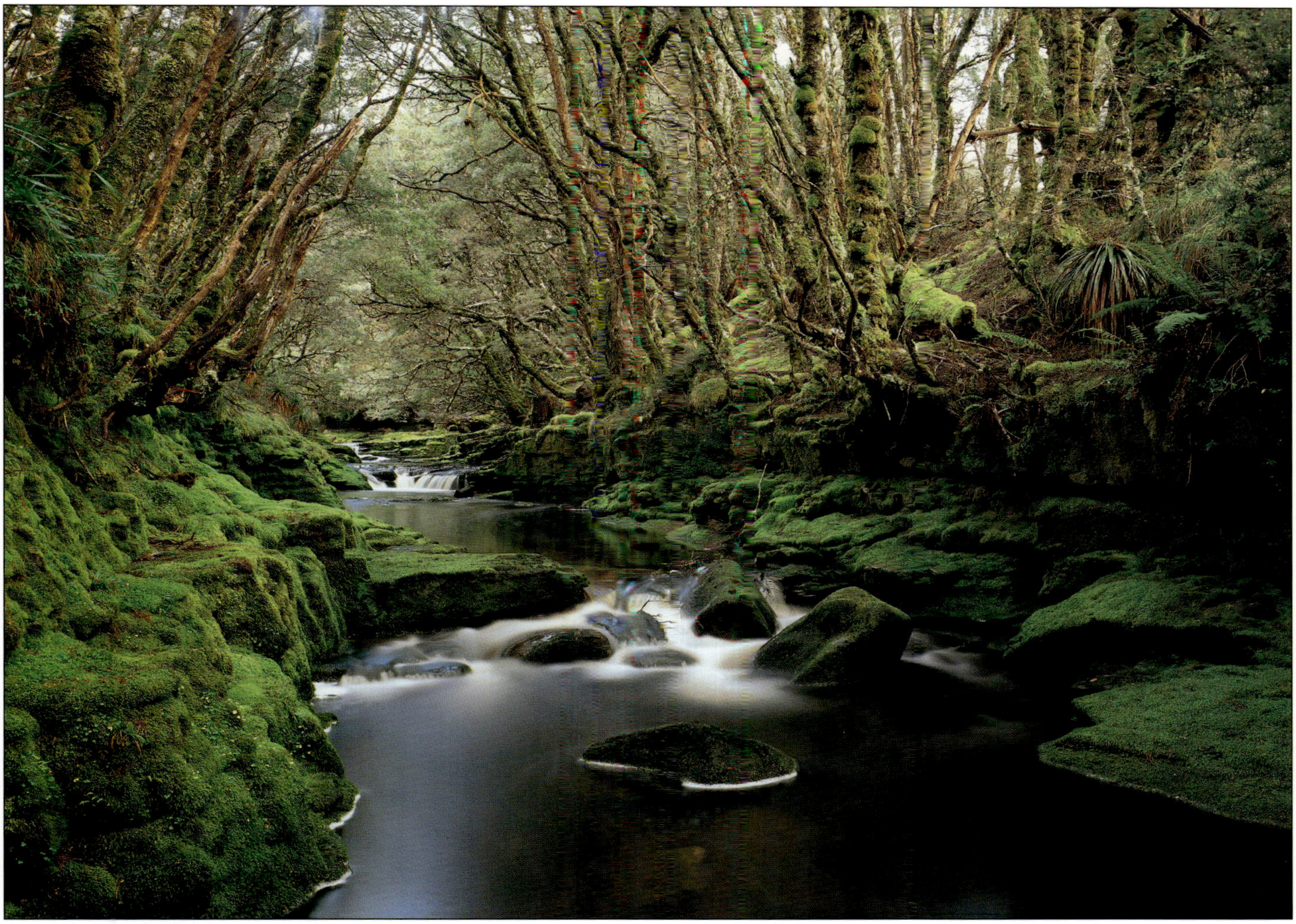

A beautiful rainforest stream, Cradle Mountain - Lake St Clair National Park.

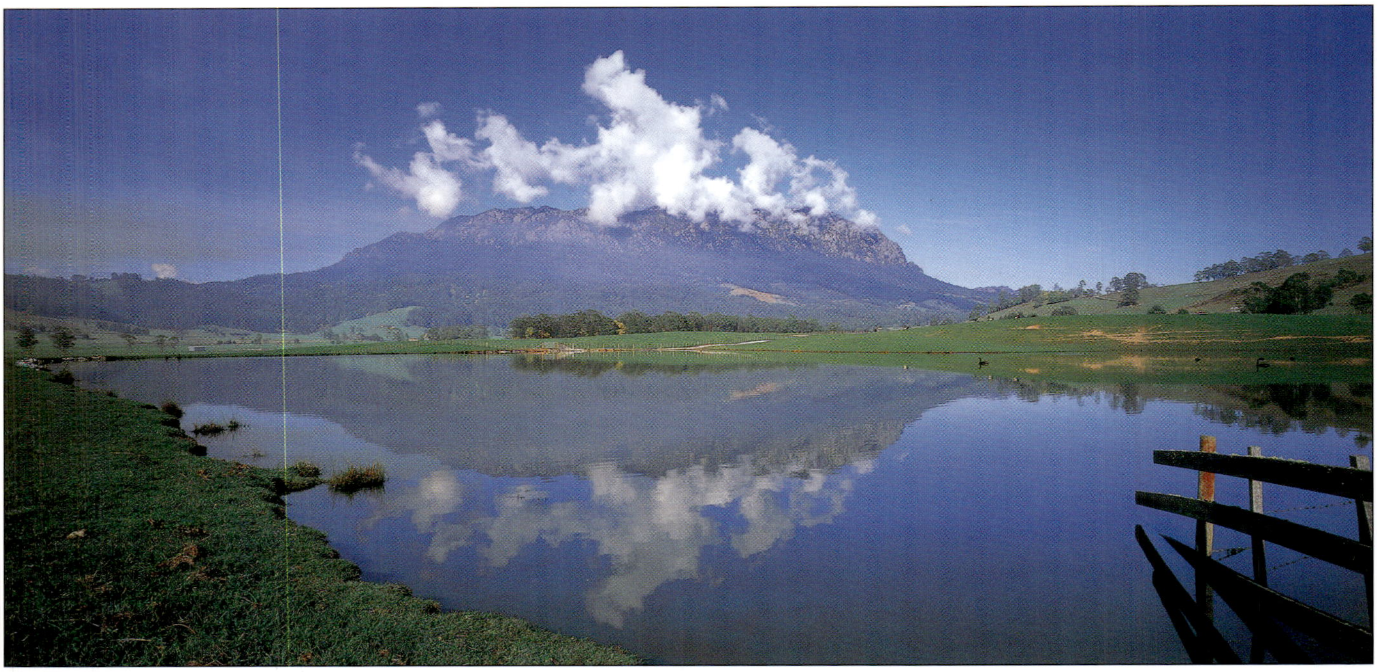

Mount Roland rises abruptly above farmland near Sheffield.

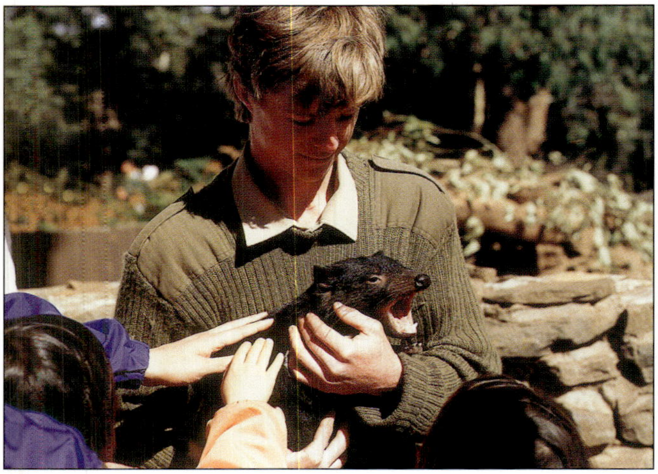

A Tasmanian devil at Trowunna Wildlife Park.

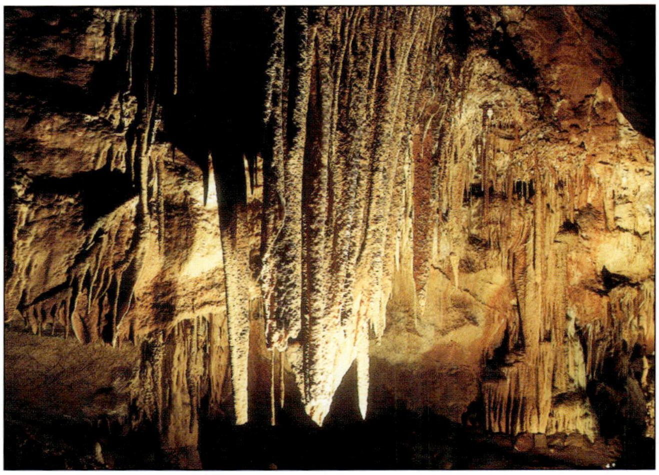

Limestone formations, Mole Creek Karst National Park.

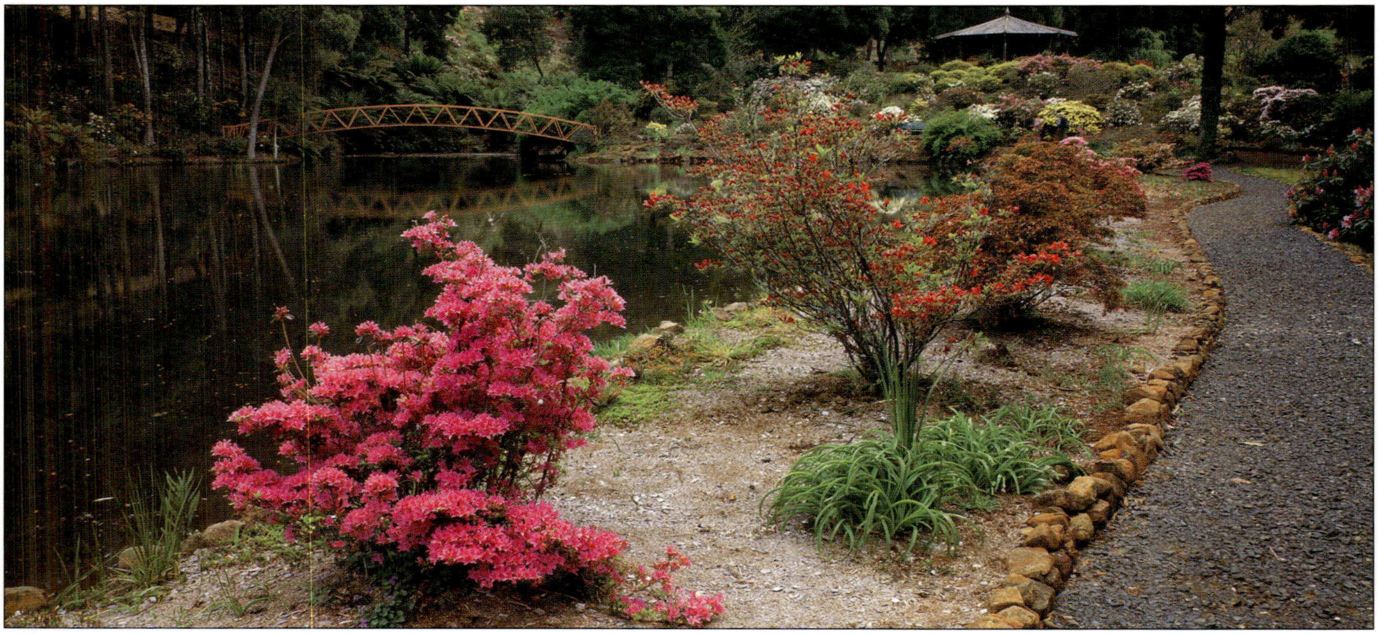

Vibrant Springtime colour, Emu Valley Rhododendron Garden near Burnie.

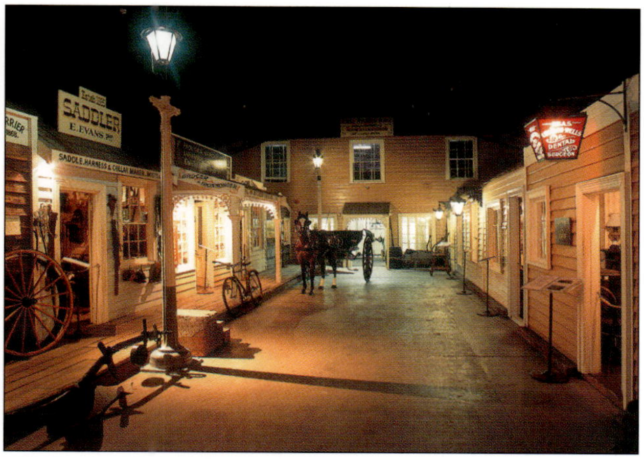

Pioneer Village Museum, Burnie.

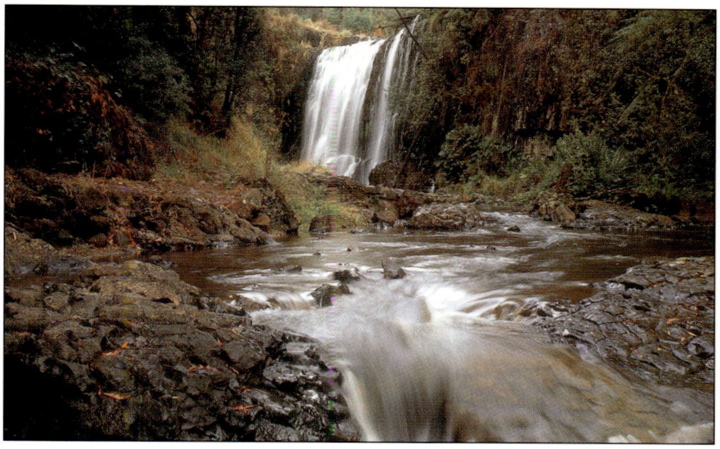

Guide Falls near Burnie.

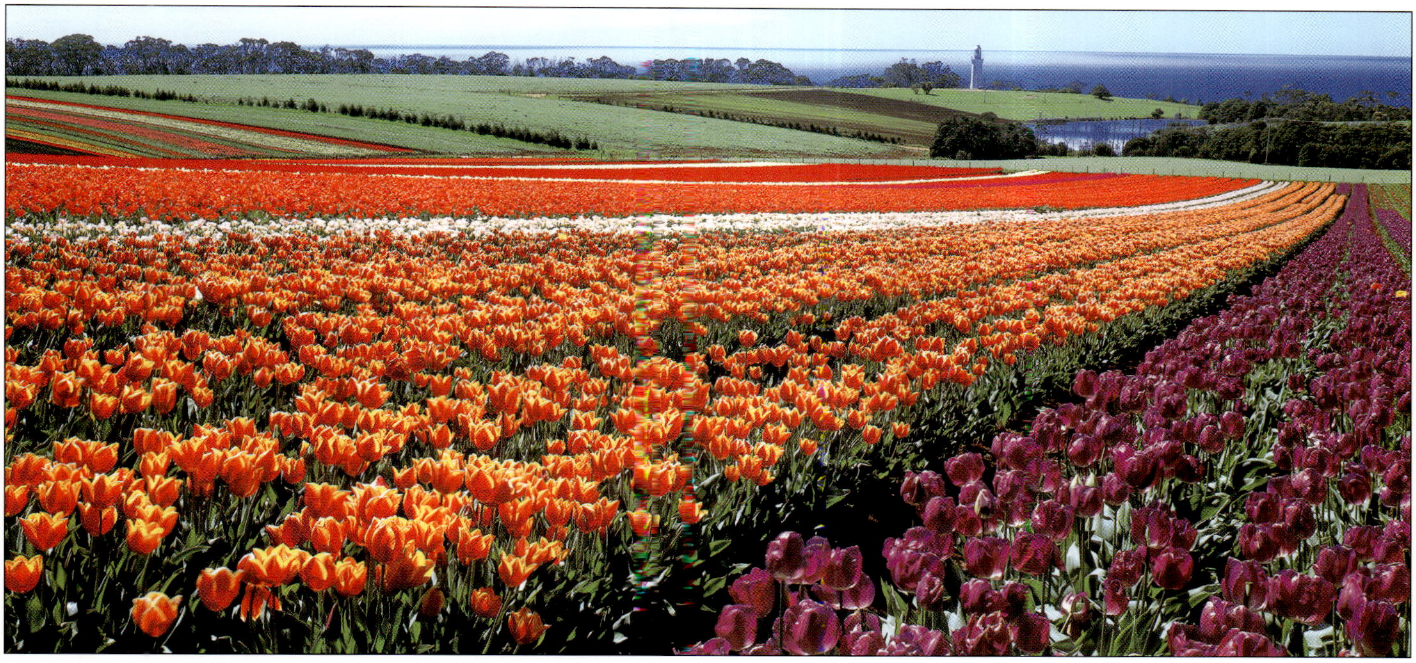

Springtime brings brilliant colour to the Table Cape Tulip Farm near Wynyard.

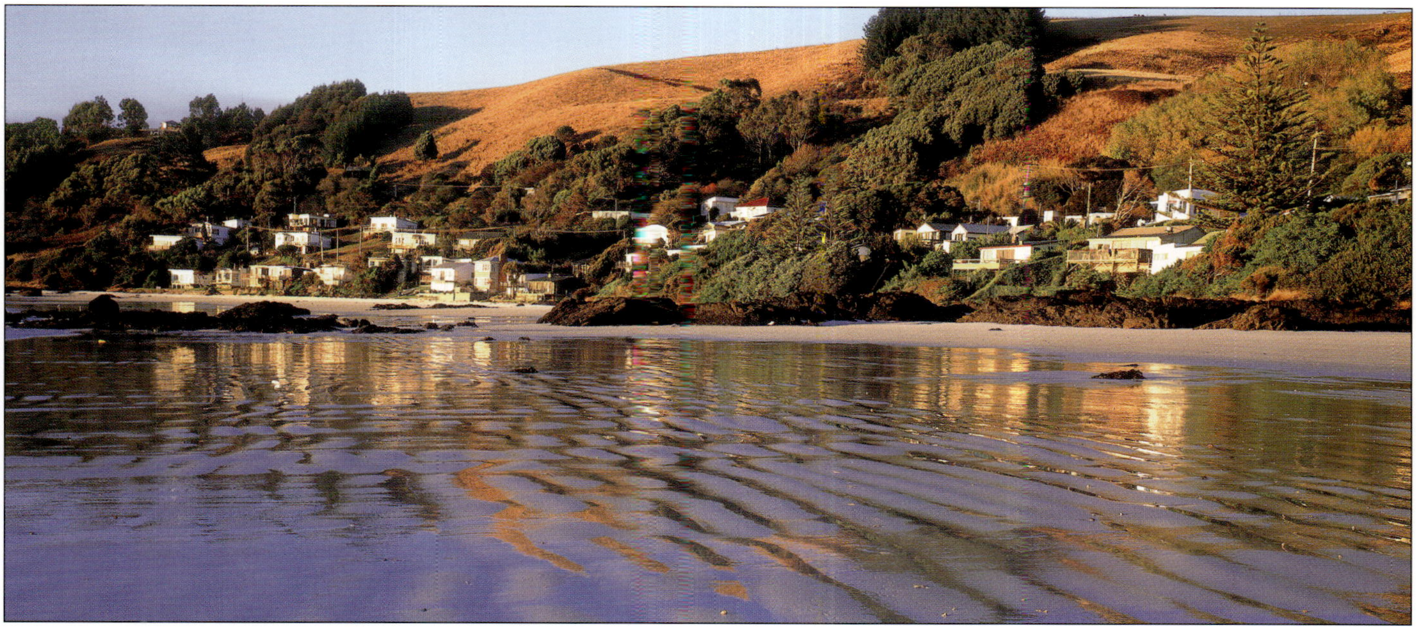

Early morning at magnificent Boat Harbour Beach.

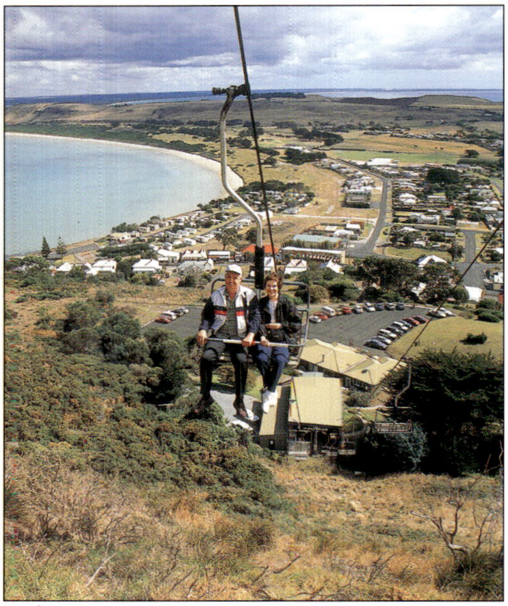
The Nut Chairlift, the easy way to the summit.

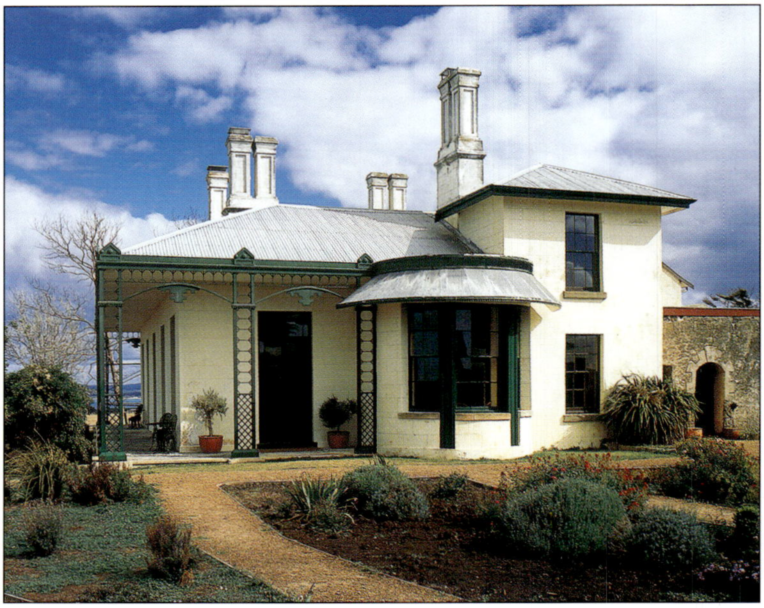
Highfield House (c. 1832), Stanley.

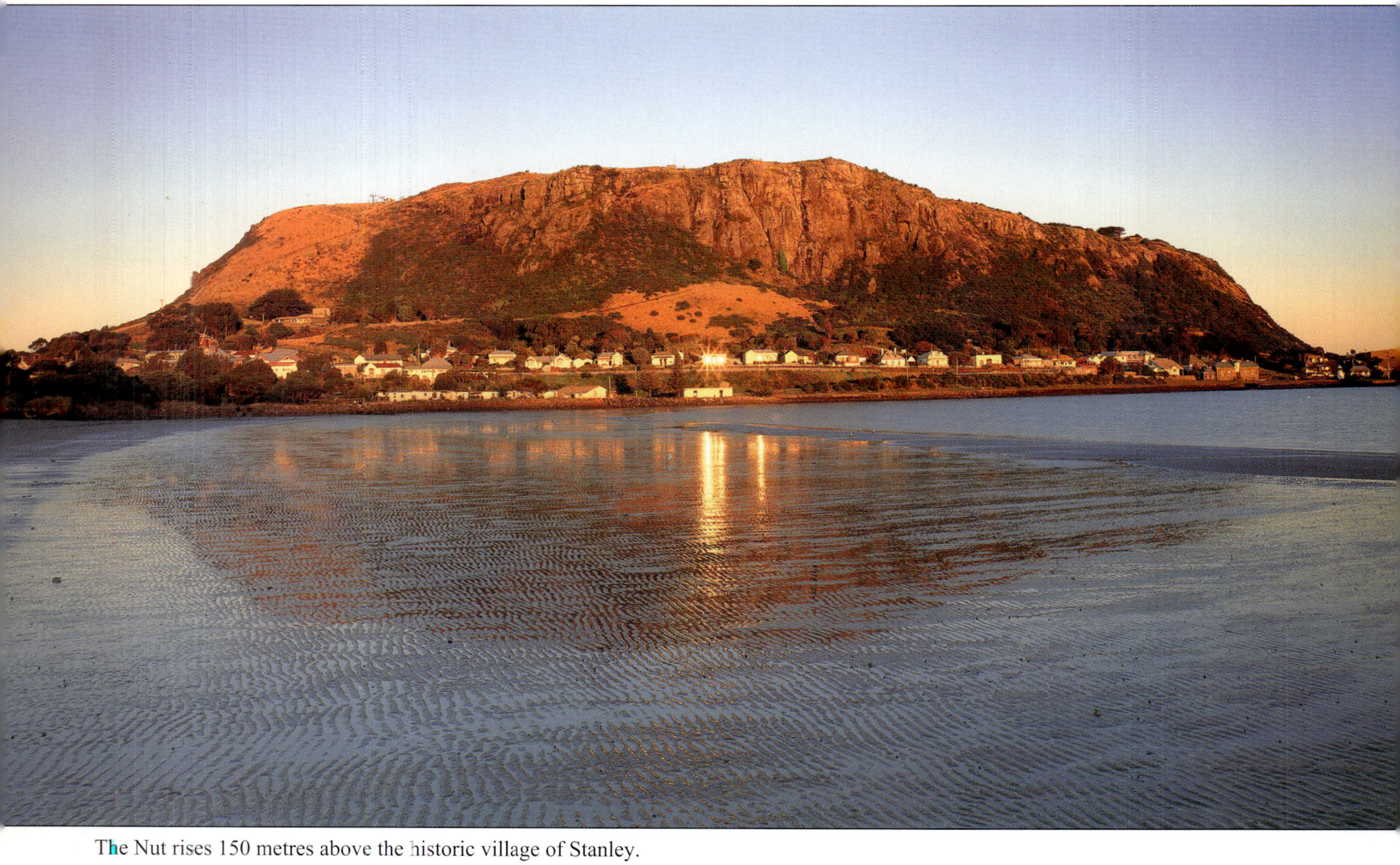
The Nut rises 150 metres above the historic village of Stanley.